D0429487

Words of praise for *unbroken*,
by Tracy Elliott

"Tracy's openness and honesty about her life is inspiring. She is an example of how, through the love and power of Jesus Christ, lives can be changed."

> — **Pat and Cheri Summerall**
> Former NFL Athlete and
> Multi-Award-Winning
> Sports Broadcaster for CBS,
> FOX, and ESPN

"Tracy Elliott is living proof that through strong faith in Christ one can overcome trial and tribulation. Tracy radiates the light of God, and I feel inspired after being in her presence—that all things are possible through Christ our Lord."

> — **Janine Turner**
> Actress

"Tracy and her family are very spiritual and generous people, a fact made much more meaningful when you know where she was from and what she had to deal with growing up. This book shows us where she got the strength and ability to raise her family in such a positive and loving way. They are role models for our generation."

> — **Jacob Arabo**
> Jeweler, Jacob & Company,
> New York

"Tracy Elliott's book, *unbroken*, is a must-read for every person who has been wounded by life. In this powerful, life-changing book, Tracy's story is proof that it is not what happens to you in life that matters most, but what happens in you. *Unbroken* will not only impact your life, but it will inspire you to turn any adversity you face into an advantage for your success."

— **Keith A. Craft**
President, Leadership
Shapers Institute; Corporate
Coach, Senior Leader,
Celebration Covenant
Church, Frisco, Texas

"Meeting Tracy was definitely divine intervention. Her message of faith brought my husband and me back to the Lord. For that, we will be forever grateful."

— **Tracy Crist**
Executive Director,
Mrs. Texas Pageant

"*Unbroken* is the riveting story thousands of beautiful women need to hear about the real God. Not the religious, harsh, and angry one, who is preached in many pulpits across this country, but the one who is loving and forgiving and truly cares more about people than their performance. Tracy Elliott's *unbroken* is the healing balm for many who have endured the pain of sexual and verbal abuse."

— **Robert Morris**
Senior Pastor at Gateway
Church in Southlake, Texas;
Author of the best-selling
book *From Dream to Destiny*

"My wife and I first met Tracy and Bryan three years ago. It is a true testament to the power of God for her to go through all that she's been through and persevere to be the beautiful, caring person we know and love."

— **Mark McLemore**
19-year Major League
Baseball Veteran and ESPN
analyst

"Tracy's story is uplifting and inspirational, not only because of the incredible odds she had to overcome, but also because of the inimitable wit and charm she displays in telling it. It is gripping and disturbing, but also funny and triumphant, and truly an example of how one's faith can help overcome the most difficult odds and help to keep striving for all the miracles that life has to offer."

— **Benedict Coulter**
Co-Founder/President of
Trailer Park Inc.,
Hollywood, California

"My prayer is that by Tracy telling her story tormented children and women around the world will find the courage and hope to believe there is a brighter future if they just hang on and place their trust in the same redeeming God that Tracy did. I only hope you are as profoundly touched by reading this story as I have been."

— **Mike Hayes**
Pastor Covenant Church
Carollton, Texas

unbroken

by Tracy Elliott

with Jenna Glatzer

ROCK SPRINGS LIBRARY
SWEETWATER COUNTY LIBRARY SYSTEM
ROCK SPRINGS, WYOMING

THOMAS NELSON
Since 1798

thomasnelson.com

READER ADVISORY: DUE TO THE NATURE OF THIS MEMOIR, THE TEXT OF THE BOOK CONTAINS SOME GRAPHIC LANGUAGE AND SITUATIONS. WHILE CARE HAS BEEN TAKEN TO MINIMIZE THESE ELEMENTS, SOME ARE NECESSARY SO THAT THE TRUE NATURE OF THE AUTHOR'S EXPERIENCES CAN BE SHARED.

This is the author's true story, but in some instances the sequence of events, identities, and descriptions of some of the people have been changed to protect their privacy.

Copyright © 2007 by Tracy Elliott

All rights reserved. No portion of this book may be reproduced, stored in a retrieval system, or transmitted in any form or by any means—electronic, mechanical, photocopy, recording, scanning, or other—except for brief quotations in critical reviews or articles, without the prior written permission of the publisher.

Published in Nashville, Tennessee, by Thomas Nelson, Inc.

Nelson Books titles may be purchased in bulk for educational, business, fund-raising, or sales promotional use. For information, please e-mail SpecialMarkets@ThomasNelson.com.

Library of Congress Cataloging-in-Publication Data

Elliott, Tracy.
    Unbroken / by Tracy Elliott ; with Jenna Glatzer.
      p. cm.
    ISBN-13: 978-0-7852-2167-8 (hardcover)
    ISBN-10: 0-7852-2167-0
    1. Elliott, Tracy. 2. Christian biography. I. Glatzer, Jenna. II. Title.
BR1725.E463A3 2007
277.3'083092—dc22
  [B]   2006037787

Printed in the United States of America

1 2 3 4 5 6 QW 10 09 08 07

Bryan, Jacob, and Elijah:

This may be my book, but this is our story.

Without you, there would be no meaning to the title.

Thank you for believing in me.

As for me and

my house, we will

serve the Lord.

— *Preface* —

I'M NOT A TEACHER, OR A PREACHER, OR A DOCTOR with all the answers about how to cure what ails you. I'm just a person with a story. It's a story I hope will inspire you, and maybe help you see the world a little differently from when you started.

Lots of people have stories, but not all of them are willing to tell theirs. It takes some courage to expose things you've spent most of your life trying to block out. But if there's something I've learned in life, it's that shame is worthless. There are parts of my life I'd rather forget, and decisions I made that weren't very good, but there's nothing I'm ashamed to talk about. All of it led me to where I am today, which is a good place. I'm a wife and mother, a successful businesswoman, Mrs. Texas, and now an author. And I've barely gotten started!

There are a couple of things I'd like to tell you before we go further. First, I want you to know that my life wasn't always pretty, so there are some things in this book that may seem a little harsh. That's because it's the truth. To give you a real picture of what it was like to grow up in a world of abuse and addiction, I needed to stay faithful to the language that was really used and the events that took place. There's nothing in this book meant for shock value.

Second, I want you to understand that this is not a self-help book, and I don't intend for anyone to think I'm going to try to tell you how to live your life. It's easy to be a Monday morning quarterback when the football game was on Sunday, but it's not up to anyone else to decide what's right for you. I feel very fortunate to be in a place in my life where I'm able to share my story and know that I'm okay with whatever comes of it, knowing that not everyone will see things the way I see them. The last thing any one of us needs is to have other people judge us when they haven't lived in our shoes.

One of the ongoing themes in my life and in this book is that God loves everyone no matter what, and no one is beneath his grace or unforgivable in His eyes. He loves us in spite of anything we could do wrong, and He loves us more than we can imagine. Even when we can't see past the next hour or the next day, He has an amazing destiny for each of us, too. You are called to do things that only you can do.

Your calling may not seem big, or it may feel common, and it may feel like your actions go unnoticed, but I promise that God sees it. He knows your heart and your intentions, and I am so thankful for that!

My desire is to show people, by telling my story, that God is so faithful and true, and not just to the "perfect" people. It would have been easier for me to pretend that I've always been where I am now, and that my life is flawless. That I stroll along every day singing hymns and throwing flowers. But all that pretending would get exhausting! Just as I had challenges earlier in my life, I still have challenges now, and I still make plenty of mistakes. But at the end of the day, all I need or want out of life is to know that when I stand before the Lord, and He asks me if I've done all I could do to live up to my destiny, I'll able to say yes.

Thank you for reading my book. I hope it'll find a place in your heart.

— *One* —

FOR YEARS, I THOUGHT MY MOTHER HAD DIED IN bed next to me. It was storming that night, and our rickety old house was leaking and creaking, and she was dying. I knew it. I knew it ever since her boyfriend and I took her to the doctor, and he told her that if she didn't quit drinking, she would die.

"Do you understand?" he asked her.

"I understand."

When we got back to the car, her boyfriend asked where she wanted to go.

"To the liquor store."

I screamed at her then in my mind, a mix of fury and tears. *Didn't you hear? He said you would die! He just said . . .*

Thunder shook the house, and I was alone with her now, six years old and scared. My uncle stopped by earlier that day, and when he saw my mom, he went to get my grandmother. He knew, too.

I know all kids think their moms are the most beautiful women in the world, but my mom was stunning—the kind of woman who made people stop in the streets and stare. Petite, so well put together all the time, with her purse over her arm and her magnetic smile. I always hoped I would look just like her when I grew up.

But Mom didn't look like Mom anymore. She was yellow. Jaundice is what they call it—one of the symptoms of cirrhosis of the liver. But I just knew that the more I saw her skin and eyes turn yellow, the more I was losing her, and the devil was winning. She was tired all the time and throwing up blood clots the size of hand towels. I'd try to help her to the bathroom, but she didn't always make it in time. Sometimes she didn't make it out of the bed. She'd try to clean the blood off her face and the blankets, and I'd make an effort to help.

It's funny the little details you remember about things that turn your life upside-down, even when the big details are too hard to think about. For me, it's the *Dennis the Menace* coloring book. I wanted to comfort her, so I brought her my coloring book and turned it to a page where Dennis's mom is wearing a flowered housecoat and fixing him breakfast. Pink was my mom's favorite color, so that's the crayon I gave her, but she couldn't stay in the lines.

That drove me crazy. The whole page was a scribbled mess, no matter how I tried to help her. So I yelled at her to stay in the lines. This strange rage built up inside, and I was trying to be angry about her coloring even though I was really angry about her dying.

"Tracy, Momma's too weak to color," she said.

My drunk uncle drove my grandmother over, and I remember Mom and I going back to her house that night. Grandma had two beds: one twin and one queen-size, and I crawled in the big bed with my mom and kissed her goodnight. The next memory I had was waking up the next morning and sensing that I was late for school.

I heard these voices coming from another room—my relatives from far away. Why were they all there? Something was wrong. I walked out into the living room, and everyone was just staring at me. I went straight over to my grandma, who grasped my hands.

"I have something to tell you," she said. "Your mom died last night."

I ran into the bathroom and closed the door. My brother Dave, who's six years older than I am, hid in the bedroom. My brother Bobby, who's ten years older than I am, just left the house. That about summed up the way we would live for the next several years.

Bobby's the one who told me that I was remembering wrong. I thought it was all one night—the storm, the coloring book, then my aunts' voices in the living room. But it wasn't.

"She lived for two weeks after that," he said. "We took her to the hospital that night."

I liked my version better. The real one, which came back to me in a torrent as he spoke, was uglier. We did take her to the hospital that night, and that's where she would stay. It was a little hospital in a little bitty southern town. I never wanted to visit, but they made me. There were tubes up her nose, all kinds of machines, her hair was a wreck, and her stomach was swelled out like she was eight months pregnant.

One day she opened her eyes, and I asked, "Are you having another baby?" I didn't know why that made her cry so much.

The nurses later told me that they could hear her crying down the hall after I left, calling out that she was sorry about the bad choices she made. But it was too late. Bobby was sixteen at the time, and he was the one who saw her final breath. For two weeks, he didn't leave that hospital because he never wanted her to be alone. He had to take the wedding ring off her finger before they brought her to the morgue.

Country people really make the most of their mourning. They can have a funeral that lasts for a week. I didn't want any part of it, but there I was in my nicest dress in the front row, on display for everyone to hug and pat on the head.

"That bloated woman in the coffin isn't my mom," I wanted to tell them. "My mom is the woman who used to tell me to grab the shampoo so we could wash our hair out in the rain. She's the one who took us to pecan orchards and didn't even mind when I decided to lie on the pecan sacks and get a tan while she and my brothers did all the work. When she made my sandwiches, I didn't want to eat the crust, but she told me the crust would make me pretty, so I ate it!" We had happy times. Things could have been different.

But instead, there she was, and now she would live at the funeral home with my dad the way she wanted to. That's what I told my school friends because that's what I thought: My parents would always be together in the funeral home now.

My dad had died of a massive heart attack when he was thirty-eight and I was two. He just went to get the newspaper, then walked back into the room and fell down. I was playing on the floor, and he just collapsed right next to me. I remember thinking he was just asleep, but my mom was hysterical, and Bobby ran next door to get the neighbor, who was a doctor. On his way out, he didn't have time to bother with the latch on the screen door, so he completely broke the door down getting out. I think they were able to revive my dad for a minute, but he died on the way to the hospital.

I'm not supposed to remember him, but I do. I remember his face, his charm. I remember he wasn't very nice to my mom, and I remember how much she loved him anyway.

Just recently, I took all our old reel-to-reel family movies and had them converted to DVD. I hadn't seen many of them before, and many of them were taken before I was born. The funny thing is the progression. I could barely remember a time when my mom wasn't frazzled and drinking all the time, so it was an eye-opener for me.

In the earlier scenes, it's like you're looking at the Cleaver family. They're all clean cut, wearing nice clothes. My dad has the hair and facial features of a young Elvis, and my mother's hair is always done. You can see how in love they were and how cute they could be with each other. By the time I was born, they looked totally different. Not put together at all. And in those last few years, my dad ended up looking like the older Elvis—heavy and bloated and used up.

What happened to these people? It's like the Cleavers accidentally got on a Rolling Stones tour bus and never got off. The American Dream expiring and curdling like bad milk right before my eyes.

There's no sound in any of the movies, but you can still tell when they're drunk. There's one that just makes my heart crack because it feels like a window into my mother's mind. My uncle, who had just come home from Vietnam, was standing in his uniform in front of the camera, drunk as can be. My mom is sewing and yelling at him. My dad is drunk, too, and she looks at him out of the corner of her eye in such a sad way, like she's thinking, "Great, I have to put up with *this* now." A minute after they shut off the camera, you know the two men were headed to a bar to meet women. That's what my family tells me about my dad, surrounded by words like, "Not to hurt your feelings about your dad, Tracy, but . . ."

I never saw him beat her, but I hear that he did. My brothers saw more of it than I did. It's one of those things that was better not to know.

My dad didn't have much family to speak of. His mom had died when he was two, and he'd lived with his grandmother, who was a little kooky. I hear that she loved him, but I don't think he ever had anyone who spoke positive things into his life. No one was telling him, "You're meant for better things than this." He and his dad hated each other, so much that my dad changed the spelling of his last name just to distance himself totally. My grandfather was an alcoholic who died homeless on the streets. That breaks my heart because I know that wasn't God's plan for him.

I never met the man, but Bobby did, once. Bobby was in a grocery store and the man who was standing behind him on line asked him if he knew our father, John. "That's my dad," Bobby said. Bobby and dad looked so much alike that it was easy to make the connection. The man said, "I'm your granddaddy." Bobby hoped for a reconciliation, but we never saw him again.

About all I know about his side of the family is that they're Cherokee Indian and that my dad had a pretty volatile and troubled youth and wound up resenting them.

So instead, he hung around with my mom's brothers, but he got into fights with all of them. My dad was six feet tall, and had a real *I can kill you if I want to* vibe. Which is why my uncles were deathly afraid of making him mad.

Before I was born, he had a three-chair barber shop. That was a really impressive thing back then in those parts. Three chairs meant you were really successful. I think my mom was able to quit working by then. She had worked her whole life. One of the places she worked was a paper mill, but now they were always taking vacations and going dancing and socializing. She loved to cook, and she threw the best birthday parties for my brothers.

If you didn't know better, you'd think theirs was the sweetest love story. My mom was twenty-five when they got married—practically a spinster in those times. Most of the women she knew were married and having kids by nineteen, but she just hadn't fallen in love. It's not like she didn't have suitors; there were plenty of men who would have given their right ears to marry my mom, but it wasn't until my dad came along that she gave away her heart. It was five years before they had my brother Bobby, so it wasn't exactly a shotgun wedding. My dad was the center of her world.

My dad was tough with my brothers, but never ugly to me. I was his angel. I followed him around and tried to imitate him. We had a dresser with a mirror attached to it, and that's where my dad would stand to comb his hair, except that he was so tall he had to squat down to see himself. So I would stand next to him and squat down when I combed my hair, too, and I would comb it straight back like he did. After he died, I kept doing it like that and my mom would walk by and cry.

To hear her relatives tell it, she wasn't an alcoholic until after he died, but you don't get cirrhosis of the liver that quickly. She always drank, but it was after his death that she became a sad drunk. Doesn't matter that he was abusive and a cheat or that she had three kids left to live for. She'd take me to the cemetery to visit his grave. Well, not exactly his grave, because it didn't have a marker, and we didn't know exactly where he was buried, but she knew the general area. Sometimes we'd sit in the parking lot. She'd just sit there and drink and cry. *What am I supposed to do to make her stop crying?* I thought. *When will it stop?* Nothing could console her, but she worked hard at finding comfort in that bottle, just like he had.

Money was a concern right away. I can remember hearing "What are we going to do?" conversations, which is why my grandmother moved us to the Projects in a small country town in the South. For a while, we lived in a very bare neighborhood with no trees. It looked like people just built low-cost housing in the middle of a field. There was nothing cozy about it; it was just bare and sad.

In the back of our house was a slab of concrete that we liked to call a porch, and on it, I had one of those little cooking sets with a pretend refrigerator, which my grandmother bought me. I was out there sweeping with my little red broom and pretending to cook one day when my brother Dave came and broke my broom. That's just how he was.

Dave and Bobby had no rules once my dad died. After he was gone, my mother didn't bother trying to tell the boys how to behave. Now that I know how young twelve years old really is, it breaks my heart that Bobby was allowed to be out past midnight. Drinking and smoking, too, I'm sure. Dave wasn't far behind.

There was a daycare center down the street, and I wanted to go to it so bad. My grandma went to work there as an assistant so I could go. I loved it so much that even thinking about it today gets me excited. The teachers were nice to me, and there was a playground there. Goats lived in a field in back of the center, and we could feed them through the fence. I was a timid girl, and I didn't smile a lot, but I remember feeling happy there.

I had a little yellow plastic toy radio that I carried around everywhere. It played "Raindrops Keep Falling on My Head," and you had to wind it up to play it. As the song played, a picture of a boy and girl in rain boots circled around. My mom bought it for me and I would sing along with it. We all liked to sing. Bobby would sing "Jeremiah Was a Bullfrog" and my mom would sing "Me and Bobby McGee."

After we moved there, my mom started getting gussied up and going to honky-tonk bars to meet men. I watched her get ready in the bathroom, blotting her lipstick on a piece of paper—which I would save and "try out" to see if the shape of my lips matched hers—then dabbing the same lipstick on her cheeks and calling it rouge. She was a good Southern woman; she wouldn't go out without makeup on, painted like a work of art. Cheap perfume, a cloud of Aqua Net hair spray, and off we went with the car swerving and jerking all the way. The lining on the roof of the car was coming unglued and hanging down, so I'd use that as an excuse to stand in the passenger seat and hold up the head-liner, with my head touching the roof. I felt like a Weeble, trying to keep my balance all the way to the bar.

She'd sit me on top of the bar and leave some nights, just drunk enough to assume I'd be fine. A cousin or aunt would sometimes come pick me up. Somehow, we always got home, but I wonder what would have happened if she lived. If she was leaving me to be watched by bartenders when I was four, what would have come next?

But my mother was good-hearted. A petite woman with thick black hair like mine, she was the one who went to work when she was just a young girl out of high school in order to help my grandmother take care of the rest of the kids at home. My grandfather had died in his fifties, so Mom did all she could to help out. When she was drunk, my mom would yell at me sometimes, but she wasn't mean on purpose. She was just pitiful.

"You look so much like your dad," she would tell me. "I miss him so much." Then she would cry for hours on end.

There were a few times I can remember when it wasn't so sad with her, mostly in the last house. We moved again to an old wooden house in the middle of nowhere on a red clay dirt road. Winter was cold because it didn't have much insulation, and it had a tin roof. I loved when it rained, because I loved to fall asleep to the sound of the rain against the tin roof. It was scary, too, though, because you really could hear *everything* in that house, and there were bobcats in the woods, and whippoorwills, crickets, and frogs. Dave and I both slept in the room with my mom because we were too chicken to sleep alone. Still, it was our house of adventure.

I learned to ride a bike on that dirt road, with my mom holding the back of the seat over and over until I finally got it right. I still have a scar on the spot where I busted my knee falling off, but she was so excited when I kept my balance that first time. It was a victory.

And she had a birthday party for me at my grandma's house when I turned six. I got to invite my kindergarten friends, my teacher, and a couple of kids who lived in the neighborhood by my grandma, and we churned home-made vanilla ice cream. Just like she did in the car on the day I got my kindergarten pictures taken, she wanted to fix the cowlick that always stuck up on the top of my hair. She licked her hand and wiped my hair down. *Eew*! I thought. My mom was already sick by then, but it was a happy memory anyway. It's the only birthday party I can ever remember having with her. She died about a month later.

She would never see what I became. Would never know that the little girl of hers would break out of the Projects and live a life most people dream about, where family would really mean something and money would never be a concern.

I know she wanted to be a good mom. Bobby knew her during the years when they weren't drunk all the time, and he worshipped her. There was a time when she lived for her family, which is what makes it so hard to accept the way things turned out. One time, a tornado barreled through our neighborhood, and Dave and I huddled under the bed. He cried like a baby, the house shaking like it was about to go flying, and my mom seemed more concerned about checking on her boyfriend than us.

When my mother was really lost in her grief, she'd just get so drunk that she'd pass out at dinnertime. I knew she was dying of a broken heart. Her soul gave up living the day my dad died, and every day was just prolonging the time until she'd join him. I don't think she just woke up one morning and decided, "I think from now on, I'll look like hell and stop caring," but she got slacker and slacker over time. She stopped doing her hair, and as she stopped caring about her own appearance, she stopped caring about mine, too. She was always tired, and started telling me, "You'll have to make your own cereal." When you're five, it feels pretty cool to get to make your own breakfast—but I soon

realized that there was nothing she ever did with enthusi-
asm again. There was nothing she did wholeheartedly . . .
except grieve.

It got to the point where I didn't want to come home from
school, so in kindergarten, I would walk to my grandmother's
house instead. My mom would pull up with liquor on her
breath and scream, "Where have you been? I've been waiting
on you!" I would hide in my grandmother's dress, and she'd
say, "Don't yell at her." My grandmother was my sanctuary.

Besides, she always had Cokes and dumplings. She went
grocery shopping once a week and always made sure to
have food for me—cake, cookies, ice cream. We didn't eat
like that at home; there wasn't always a lot of food. We
didn't starve, but sometimes we ate the same thing for days
in a row. I guess we had food stamps, but you can trade
those in for liquor if you're willing to be sneaky.

So when I learned that we three kids were going to move
in with Grandma after Mom died, I was relieved. It wasn't
until much later that I realized how tough it must have been
for a seventy-year-old woman to suddenly have a rambunc-
tious six-year-old, a twelve-year-old, and a sixteen-year-old
to care for in addition to all her own sons who still stayed
with her. But my grandmother wasn't your typical senior
citizen. She still worked as a caretaker for a woman who was
about the same age as she was. It was at one of the fanciest
houses in town, and she'd bring me along while she cooked
and cleaned.

Of course she was devastated that her daughter had just died. She cried for what my mom could have been, should have been. She cried for us and for herself, but then she had to stop mourning, because the truth was that someone had to pay for the funeral, and make phone calls, and get clothes for the kids. Things always fell into her lap, and I know she saw it coming.

I know the way she looked at my mom with sadness and frustration in her eyes, as if to say, "Get it together!" She knew she was watching her daughter kill herself and leave three kids behind. And I knew it, too. You just couldn't fool me, even when I was little. My aunts would tell me, "Your momma's just sick, Tracy . . . she'll get better," and I would think, *No, she's not going to get better because the doctor told her to quit drinking, and she's still drinking every day. She's not going to get better because she doesn't want to get better. She's not going to get better because she doesn't care, and she's killing herself so she can be with my dad!*

Why couldn't she have lived for us?

We were good children, beautiful children, and we needed her. One time, I heard her pray this sad, drunken prayer to God about her mistakes. "Please, God, forgive me for the things I've done . . ." She was raised Baptist, and I think she believed in heaven and hell, though she never took us to church.

But when she died, I think she was convinced that she was just too far gone to be redeemed. She would cry and say, "I'm a horrible mom. Look how much you love me and all the things I've done wrong." I think she believed she was going to hell, and there was nothing she could do about it anymore.

We were orphans now. And life was about to get a lot worse.

— *Two* —————————————

WHERE WERE YOU, YOU LITTLE WHORE? OUT screwing somebody?" That was what my uncle screamed in my face the first time I came home late from school when I was in the first grade. Except he used worse cuss words. "Your mom was a whore, too."

All my six uncles lived with my grandmother on and off, and five of them were violent drunks who never had jobs for any length of time. For some reason, her five daughters were all decent people, but her sons were rotten to the core. If not for them, I would have been happy staying with Grandma forever. But my uncles were a tornado of fists and hate, abuse of every stripe. Just about every night, they'd get to drinking and fighting, and when I say "fighting," I mean the broken-bones-and-bloody-nose variety.

They were *really* not happy about having the three orphan kids move in. Sympathy wasn't exactly their strong suit, but they had no problem with resentment.

ROCK SPRINGS LIBRARY
SWEETWATER COUNTY LIBRARY SYSTEM
ROCK SPRINGS, WYOMING

17

"You're here living off my momma!" one would say, and I'd think, *But I'm six. You're forty and you're living off your momma.*

"You're lucky we let you live here. Our momma has to put up with having to take care of you because your momma was so stupid."

It wasn't like that when they were sober. When they were sober, they were downright decent to us. The problem is that they were almost never sober. Out of a month, they'd spend about three weeks drunk and maybe one week sober. They would go on binges where they'd be drunk from morning until night literally for weeks at a time, then they'd sober up long enough to get an odd job for one week—long enough to get one paycheck. During tobacco season, they might get hired to pick tobacco or do other farm chores; otherwise, it was mostly construction jobs or painting. They'd take their checks straight to the liquor store and bail out of work the next morning. Maybe they meant to go back, but once they were drunk, they were drunk for weeks and couldn't get it together to finish the jobs.

It got to the point where no one wanted to hire them even for the worst jobs no one else wanted, because the employers knew what was going to happen. In a small town, there aren't many secrets, and everyone knew what my uncles were going to do with their work money. Sometimes someone would say to my grandma, "I could have really used Ronald to help me last week, but I didn't want to help him get drunk and lay up over at your house."

It was a real bittersweet thing when they worked. I knew I'd get a one-week reprieve from their drunken horror show, because they'd stay sober for that first week on the job—so that was great. But I also knew it was going to be a lot worse as soon as they had money. It meant that they could binge even worse than before until the money ran out and they had to start the cycle again.

White port is what they drank, mostly. It was a cheap wine with a long, skinny neck, and they would put it in paper bags to cover up the labels. If they were coming off a long drunk and having delirium tremens (DT), they would drink beer to get through the withdrawal. But in lean times, they'd drink literally anything that could give them a buzz. At Christmas time, Grandma used to pray aloud that no one would give them cologne, because they'd just drink it. "Please, no Old Spice this year." You couldn't keep it in the house—rubbing alcohol, Nyquil, anything that could intoxicate them. Honest to goodness, they'd drink it.

This was a group activity. They all fed off each other, like they were powerless to refuse if one person decided it was time to drink.

"I hope so-and-so doesn't come over," one would say. "He's been riding all over town drunk for three weeks." They all knew that they didn't have the willpower to say no if the drunken one showed up and said, "Let's go for a ride."

All the furniture in the house was beat-up hand-me-down anyway, but piece by piece, it all got wrecked, except this one old wooden china cabinet in my grandmother's kitchen, which somehow remained standing despite all odds. One uncle would slam the other against the wall, smashing his back into a picture frame that would leave shattered glass raining across the floor. They'd throw dinner plates at each other's heads like Frisbees, smashing them to bits. The next night, one would get revenge by body-slamming another into the kitchen table. Someone would give us a new table, and the cycle would repeat. Food would go flying, and just to make me feel small sometimes, my uncles told me to eat it off the floor like a dog.

Even though my brother Bobby wasn't a church-goer at the time, he always prayed. One night, just after he prayed over his food, my uncles smashed the table again in another fit of rage. Bobby's plate of spaghetti landed on the floor with the grace of a swan, untouched and perfectly intact. We couldn't stop laughing. We knew it was because he prayed over it. God was making a statement!

My brothers weren't around much. Dave kept getting sent to boys' homes for one trouble after another, and Bobby was a teenager who had a life of his own. He would pick up construction jobs out of town and be gone for stretches at a time, but he was there when it was important. The Christmas after our mom died, he hitchhiked home in the rain to bring presents for Dave and me because he was worried we wouldn't have any. He had our presents wrapped in tin foil so they wouldn't get wet. I don't remember what he bought Dave, but I remember that with the money he made, he bought me a tape recorder and a Big Bird activity book. How many sixteen-year-old boys would hitchhike two hundred miles in the rain to bring presents to their little brother and sister?

I never felt like I knew Dave well. He seemed to be stuck in an emotional breakdown permanently. Bobby was the best protector he could be, even if he wasn't always around.

I couldn't exactly blame Bobby for not wanting to be there. He probably caught the worst of it from my uncles, and he tells me it's because our dad humiliated them so much. Our dad was at the top of the pecking order—if they showed up drunk at his house and started trouble, he could and would whip them. Bobby remembers a time when my uncle Len hid under the bed because my dad was on a rampage. I mean, a grown man hiding under the bed! It must have been humiliating to get caught by my brother like that.

So the first thing Len did once we moved in was to beat up Bobby. It was as if he was saying, "I couldn't whip your dad, but I can sure whip you."

They talked trash about my dad as soon as he died, even to my mother. They would tell her what an SOB he was, how he would get drunk and pick up women, and she would say, "You were with him when he did that stuff!"

But it was really game-on after she died. Then there was no one to stop them from saying hateful things, or taking out all their jealousy and embarrassment on my brothers and me. When they were really in need of an ego boost, they'd go beat up Dave.

"Quit hitting him! He's just a baby!" my grandma would yell. Twelve years old, and getting beat up by drunk men in their forties. Sometimes they would even wake my brothers out of a dead sleep just to start a fight. They'd snatch the boys right off the couch or out of bed and just start yelling.

I started getting migraines when I was four. I remember them getting worse after we moved. When I'd come home from school, my grandma would ask, "How are you feeling?" I would say "Okay," and she would look at my eyes and say, "Tracy, go lie down." The light hurt, so I'd look sadly at my friends outside, then draw the curtains shut and lie across the bed with a trash can next to me, sick as a dog. Little kids aren't supposed to get migraines. I know mine were tripped off by stress, though. Little kids aren't supposed to live with men like my uncles.

My uncles survived off my Social Security checks and my grandmother's earnings, never enough for them to move out of the Projects, but apparently enough to buy plenty of liquor to keep them going month to month. When they were short on cash, they'd sell anything that wasn't nailed down in the house. Ridiculous things, like the window fans. They'd walk down the street with the window fan and try to sell it to people along the way to the pawn shop.

Things would just disappear from the house, and my grandma would say, "I don't know what happened to it."

"Ronald or Len probably pawned it," someone would say, and the men would deny it even after they were totally caught.

"Ann saw you walking down the street with it!" my grandma would say a few days later, and they'd still act like they had no idea what she was talking about. But they had the money for their wine.

She didn't stop them. She couldn't stop them. She always made sure they were taken care of, so she'd ask what they wanted when she went to the grocery store. They'd tell her to pick them up coffee and cigarettes, and she would.

We had to walk to the grocery store. It was a long walk for an old woman trying to keep a little girl's attention, and when we got there, she would reward me by buying Coca-Colas in bottles and caramels with sugar in the middle.

On cold days, she would open the oven door, turn on the pilot light, and set my shoes on the inside of the oven door so my feet would be warm when I slipped them on. She'd also put my clothes in the dryer before I got dressed, so everything would be freshly warm. If my uncles weren't drinking, sometimes she'd bring my breakfast into the living room while I watched cartoons, and it was always a full breakfast: eggs, grits, ham, biscuits. All I wanted was Captain Crunch, which I could eat until the roof of my mouth was raw, but she used to say, "You can't eat Captain Crunch every meal!" I didn't even know then how good I had it to have a grandma cooking me such big meals all the time.

One of her specialties was layer cake. Nobody makes them now like she used to. They'd have about ten layers, and she'd put each layer on wax paper while she made her homemade chocolate icing. I'd always get to lick the icing off the beaters.

My relatives would comment on how spoiled I was and how my grandma would wait on me hand and foot. I think she did that to compensate for the way it was the rest of the time, when my uncles were drunk.

I didn't get in trouble for anything. There was a blackberry bush out in the back of our yard, and over and over, Grandma would tell me not to play back there. She was worried I'd get bitten by a snake or something. But of course, that's the first place I went. I'd pick blackberries and put them in my shirt, eating them one by one before I got back to the house.

"Have you been eating blackberries again?" she'd ask.

"No, Ma'am!" I'd say, and she'd pretend not to notice the giant purple stain in the middle of my T-shirt.

My grandmother was maybe five foot five. She wore silver-framed glasses, pointed on the ends, and had gray, wavy hair and a round belly. Her legs were short, and you could never really tell what the rest of her looked like because she always wore long cotton house dresses that sort of just hung on her, and they were always buttoned all the way up. She was very conscious of that, making sure her brassiere never showed. I helped her get dressed a lot of the time.

I also had to help her get her earrings in. She got her ears pierced for the first time at age seventy-one, because I was seven and I wanted to get mine done. We got them done together, but she could never get hers in, so she'd ask me, "Could you help me get my earbobs in?"

She looked so sweet—angelically sweet—but you could see that she'd had a hard life. She looked beaten down and nervous all the time. You could see it in her hands; she was always wringing them together or clutching her pocket-book for dear life. In my brother's car, she would ride with one hand holding the dashboard and the other grasping her pocketbook.

"Grandma, nobody's going to come in here and take your pocketbook," Bobby would say with a grin.

"Do I look like I'm not comfortable?" she asked. "I'm comfortable. I'm comfortable!"

But she never looked at ease. Every night she would fall asleep watching the six o'clock news, and even when she was fast asleep on the couch, her lips were pursed together. Tense. And she never moved when she slept, flat on her back with her hands folded together on her belly

I slept in Grandma's bed, cuddled up with her. "When you die, I'm going to die so I can be with you," I told her.

We'd prop a chair up against the door to keep my uncles out at night. In response, they'd blast the television just to keep us awake and annoy us while they kept screaming and fighting.

The mental abuse was unreal. My grandmother would tell me to ignore them, but they were so close I could feel their breath on my cheeks when they cussed at me. "Just pretend you don't hear them and they won't bother you," she'd say, like she was teaching me how to train a misbehaving puppy. But how could I pretend? I could feel their spit. They'd get right up inches away from my face.

"Bitch" and "whore" were their favorite words, and "shut up" was mine. I'd say it very, very quietly whenever they started in on me, and if they heard me, it would just escalate. "Don't you talk to me like that! I'm grown! You're just a little bitch."

Grandma threatened to wash my mouth out with soap if I ever said "shut up" again. I couldn't believe it. It was as if she was deaf to everything they were saying to me . . . it was okay for them to call me the most profane names they could think of, but I couldn't say "shut up"? I never even cussed, which is a miracle. Most kids repeat what they hear, which means I should have had a mouth like a truck driver by the first grade.

I knew that what they were saying was wrong. I knew I wasn't all those horrible things they called me, but that didn't stop it from hurting. Sometimes the words would become more than words. My uncles would touch me and it would make me very afraid.

For most of my childhood, I slept with a Bible in my pillowcase to ward off the nightmares that never seemed to let up. But for several nights, another instrument joined the Bible under my pillow: my grandmother's sharpest butcher knife. I planned exactly how and where I would put the knife on my uncle's throat if he came into my room.

If I do this, I thought, *I have to do it for real. I have to kill him, or he'll kill me.*

Every night, I prayed for all my uncles to die, but I never fantasized about killing the rest of them myself—just the uncle who sexually abused me. I studied the veins in his throat.

What stopped me wasn't any sense that it was wrong. I thought he needed to be killed for all the horrible things he had done to my grandmother and me. But I worried that I would go to jail and never see my grandmother again. And part of me worried that she would stop loving me for killing her son.

I knew she loved me, but she chose them over me time and again, just by letting them stay there. I often wonder what my granddaddy was like, and where she learned that it was okay for her sons to treat her this way. When my granddaddy was alive, they lived on a farm in the country. He died in his fifties, though, and didn't leave anything for them. I don't know whether my uncles got worse after my granddaddy was gone, but I don't think it started with them.

This isn't to say my grandmother never stood up to them. She was a feisty woman, and I saw her hit one of them on the head with an iron frying pan and break a broom over another's head. But there was a part of her that was beat down, and it accepted all the disrespect and all the abuse.

She never touched alcohol herself, not even a glass of wine. But she also never tried to stop them from their drinking sprees. They were filthy, often wetting themselves and vomiting on themselves, and she'd just clean them up like babies. She, a woman in her seventies, managed to keep the pillowcases ironed, the house proudly clean, despite the pigs who lived there.

Why, Grandma? Why can't you just kick them out?

"When you have kids of your own, you'll understand," she'd tell me.

I don't think I will.

"You don't kick your kids out."

But they're hurting you. I saw Eddie push you down . . .

"I just fell off the step stool in the pantry is all."

She'd call them her "boys," like they were still kids, and I think she really believed that they just couldn't help themselves, and that other people were always just egging them on and making them act badly. Bobby and I would whisper to each other and roll our eyes and call them "her babies."

It could have been what happened to her first son that made her so adamant about making excuses for them. I always knew she had an older son who died, and I knew it had to be something bad that happened, because my uncles would bring him up and say, "Remember what happened to Gary," and it would make my grandma emotional. The story that I had always heard about Gary is that he had been a drinker and a fighter just like the rest of them, and she had kicked him out. So he moved to Florida and ended up getting beaten to death. She had to identify his body. That left her with a lot of guilt, and the others used that to their advantage. They could push that guilt button whenever they wanted.

Or it could've been what happened to RJ that did it. I don't know what RJ was like when he was younger. I knew him after the institution.

That was one of those family stories you never quite get to the bottom of. My grandma never talked about why he was there or how it happened, but I heard from people in the family that he was drinking like the rest of them, and my grandma didn't know what to do with him . . . so she put him in a mental institution. From all accounts, he wasn't crazy, but back then, if you went to a mental institution, the types of treatments there would *make* you crazy. I think she just wanted to put him in a place where he'd be safe, not out in the streets fighting like Gary.

She told me that when she used to go visit him, she would sleep on the bench at the bus station because she couldn't afford a hotel room.

I was told that he called my grandmother's sister and begged her to get him out of there because he was getting shock treatments, so I guess he still spoke when he left the institution, but he stopped speaking right after that. I always interpreted it as his choice—that he chose to stop speaking—although I'm not really sure if there was a physical reason. What would you have left to say if your own mother had put you away? What would there be to talk about if you felt like the whole world had turned against you?

All I know is that his presence was very calming to me. Remember I told you that five out of six uncles were lousy drunks? RJ was the exception.

Tall and slender, he had jet-black hair like mine, and he combed it straight back. It was long, but not quite shoulder length. His beard had some gray in it, and eventually his hair grayed a bit at the ends, too. He moved back in with my grandma while my mother was still alive, and I remember that even though he never spoke a word to anyone, he smiled at me when we visited.

His clothes were always the same: a white T-shirt under a white button-down cotton shirt, white painter pants, and a black belt. That's all he owned, white shirts and white pants. When he got up, he would make his bed with such perfection that it looked like a store display. He was very, very neat, and didn't like to be undressed or messy in any way, so he would sleep fully clothed—the same wardrobe, but he wore a different set of the same clothes to bed—and he would sleep on his back with his hands across his chest like a corpse, in a manner that wouldn't upset the sheets in any way. You'd never catch him all snuggled up in a blanket. He never even got under the covers. I guess that's what we'd call obsessive-compulsive disorder today.

Every day, he would sit in his room and write. He used his clothes dresser as a desk, and my grandma would have to buy him loose-leaf paper all the time. She bought 200-sheet packs, and she called them his "tablets." He would write all day and keep sharpening his pencil until it was down all the way to a nub, then he would get a new pencil. Nobody ever asked what he was writing, but my uncles sometimes gave her a hard time about wasting money.

"I don't know why you spend money buying paper and pencils when you know he's in there writing nonsense all day."

Everyone in the family seemed spooked by RJ. He was the crazy man, the haunted-house man, the man whose front door kids run away from as fast as they can. I had a cousin who I loved, Sandra, and I could never get her to go to RJ's room with me.

"He's not going to hurt you," I'd tell her. "He's fine." But she'd shake her head and say in low tones, "He's *crazy*."

I don't know why I saw him the opposite way everyone else did. He hated company, so he stuck to his room almost all the time. Really, he just came out to get food and coffee and use the bathroom, and people *never* went in his room.

They didn't even stop to wave at him. Just me. I never saw anything in him to be scared of, though. I thought he looked angelic, and he was certainly never full of rage and hate like my other uncles. So I would sit down on the corner of his bed and tell him all about my day and complain to him about my other uncles.

"Do you see them in there? Do you see how they talk? They are so stupid. They always talk like that. They knocked over the lamp today. Did you hear that when it broke?"

It was a one-way conversation, sure, but it didn't feel silly. He would smile and make little sounds and occasional gestures, then keep on writing. He understood everything, I was sure of it. And even if he didn't use words, I felt like he was very communicative. I could look in his eyes and know just what he was feeling. He wasn't one of them.

When he would walk out of his room, everything stopped. It was like a movie scene, where there's chaos all around and then someone says a magic word and everything freezes. Time stands still.

They made it seem like they were just freaked out because he was "crazy," but I think it was something different. I think they saw the goodness in him, and that's what scared them. Seeing him reminded them of how evil they had become. When he walked into the living room, they'd stop fighting in mid-punch and wait for him to pass.

They'd talk about him once his door was closed, but never to his face. "He's crazier'n a bedbug," they'd say. Just once, I wanted him to say "Boo!" to them. I think they would have all fainted.

Just once or twice, he saved me from them. I would try to break up their fights, and my grandma would yell at me not to get in the middle of them when they were swinging at each other and throwing things. They wouldn't slow down for one second, so I could easily have gone flying across the room if I walked into the wrong end of a fist.

But I'd go right up to them and try to pull them apart. When that didn't work, I'd go stand in the corner and cry and pull on my hair and say, "I can't take this anymore!" I was very seriously on the edge, crying and trying to pull my hair out and screaming, "Don't fight! Please stop it!"

"You're upsetting her," Grandma would say. "Stop doing that. Can't you see how upset she is?"

"Screw her," Len would say. "And shut up, you stupid old bitch. Nothing here concerns you."

"This is my house. Whatever you do here concerns me."

"You couldn't even live here if it wasn't for us! You just shut up."

Once, maybe twice, RJ walked out during a scene like that, plucked me up, and carried me to his room. I wished he could have stopped them all the time.

Maybe they really thought that they were contributing to the household because they sometimes gave my grandma twenty dollars to buy them coffee and cigarettes. When they were sober, they would clean the house and plant flowers for her—but they darn well should clean, considering they made the mess.

Their bedrooms smelled of body odor and masturbation. The bathrooms were spattered with bodily fluids. Grandma did the best she could, but it was like trying to clean up after zoo animals. Every time she got a room clean, someone would be in there to do something disgusting. Not that she ever gave up—she had infinite patience and would just clean it again. And again.

Something had to have happened to make them so demented, I would think. If she was such a doting mother that she would cook and clean and care for them like this when they were in their forties, then you know she was a doting mother when they were little. So what happened? Had their father done awful things to them, or to her? I'd never find out, but I'd always question how things got so dysfunctional.

Dave had learned very well that Grandma would put up with a lot of nonsense. He was sure good at writing letters. Every day, we got another letter from Dave from whatever boys' home he was in, and all the letters were the same: telling us how hard it was for him and what things he needed. Grandma was always trying to scrounge up money to buy him socks and underwear and things to take to him.

I remember when Nikes first came out, and Dave wrote a long letter saying that he wanted a pair of Nikes. My grandmother went to the shoe department in town and found out that they were really expensive. "I can't afford these," she thought, so she bought a cheaper pair of sneakers—Converse or something—and wrapped them and sent them to him.

A few days later, there was a box in our mailbox: Dave mailed the shoes back with a note that said, "I would rather not have any shoes at all." I would have let him go barefoot, but Grandma went back to the store and returned them and got the Nikes we couldn't afford and sent them to him. She let people run her down her whole life.

Thing is, though, she had a temper. It just wasn't directed at the right people, usually. And when she yelled at my uncles, she would just wind up feeling guilty about it later. They'd bring it up over and over, making it sound like she treated them bad, and she'd believe it.

I had a friend named Karen who lived nearby, and the frightening thing is that she actually liked to come over my house because it was safer than her own. She felt like it was a restful place, and she would actually cry when she wasn't allowed to stay with me. I had seen Karen's mom slap her hard across the face when we walked in and interrupted the soap opera she was watching. "Do *not* make noise when my stories are on!" she said, and she slapped the girl so hard that her cheek was red. That woman was meaner than anybody.

I was a serious-looking girl with dark hair, and Karen was a round-faced kid with curly red hair and freckles. We were a funny pair. She was intimidated by the other kids who went to the private school just outside of town; they made comments about people like us who were "slumming it" in public school, and she would take it personally. I was better at letting stuff like that roll off my back.

Karen was about the only person who would sit in RJ's room with me. We'd sit there and talk our silly seven-year-old talk, making up stories and giggling.

My story—which I really came to believe—was that I was actually a princess, and I somehow got stuck in the wrong family. Very regularly, I told myself that I had just gotten lost from my kingdom somehow and that my real family was coming to find me. My real parents weren't dead. I didn't have any disgusting, nasty uncles. I was just somehow in the wrong place at the wrong time, and any day now, a butler would come and apologize for the mistake and I would wave my princess wave and go off in a carriage to the castle that I was sure was waiting for me somewhere.

That's why I loved playing games like Candyland. I wanted to live in Candyland. I wanted to slide down the Gum Drop Trail. I wanted to find Willy Wonka's golden ticket and be Wonder Woman and live in a Judy Blume book. Every child fantasizes about these things, but probably not to the extent that I did.

Getting my library card was a major boon for me. I'd ride my bicycle to the library and spend half the day there, gathering up books to put into my basket. It would be so weighed down that I'd have trouble steering. Back in my room, I'd sit and read for hours, getting lost in the stories.

Grandma told me I could always take out books as long as I returned them on time, so I made sure to. It felt like an honor to even get to bring them home.

I was always trying to make potions and concoctions, things I read about in books. Inspired by Thomas Rockwell's *How to Eat Fried Worms*, I set out to steal Grandma's frying pan. She fried chicken in an iron pan every Sunday, and I managed to sneak it out while she was napping, along with a container of meal and the ketchup and mustard. Karen and I made a fire outside with one of my uncle's lighters and some sticks and branches we gathered. We put the worms in the container of meal and shook them up to get them good and covered. Then I stuck the worms in the frying pan, fried them up, and tried to get Karen to try one. She wouldn't.

When my grandma caught us, she was so grossed out. "Tracy, I cook in this pan! And did you have to put the worms into the container?" She could never stay mad at me, though.

One year, someone gave me Sea Monkeys. I put them in a plastic tank in the living room, because that's where Sea Monkeys go. And I put that packet of dried up little dots into the water and fed them and waited and watched and waited and watched. And soon . . . there were all these little Sea Monkeys! In my mind, there was a Mommy Sea Monkey and a Daddy Sea Monkey, and little children. I watched them swimming around and I made up stories about their little shrimpy lives and I loved them.

And then my uncles fought one night and knocked the tank over and the Sea Monkey family spilled to the floor and died. I was hysterical, screaming and trying to scoop them up and scrape them off the floor and put them back into water, fast, fast! None of them made it. And I just fell apart, because this was what I wanted my family to be. They were my pets, but they were also my model family, getting along so peacefully in their happy little tank. Like a scaled-down, aquatic version of my royal princess family that was going to find me someday, somehow.

There were pieces of my life I would have wanted to keep. My grandma, for one. She was cuddly and good, and I would have wanted to take her away with me to the castle and treat her to all the finest things and watch her be pampered. And I had a cousin who I loved, and Bobby, and Karen, and RJ. They could all come with me. The rest of my life could just sink into the moat.

This is not where I belong, I thought. *These people are wrong for what they do to me. I'm not one of them, and I'm never going to be like them.*

Little did I know.

— *Three* —

I'M STILL NOT SURE HOW I ENDED UP AT CHURCH in the first place, but I think it's that the pastor came to my grandmother's house after my mother died and invited us to come. He drove the church bus on Sunday mornings to pick up people who couldn't drive there. I'd wait outside for him, and we'd pick up other people along the way.

It was a very southern Baptist church just a couple of blocks away, and all the really important people in town were there. They all sat in the front with their very important kids, and I sat in the back because I was the orphan with the raggedy clothes who lived in the Projects. In a small town like that, everybody knew that I was the one with the crazy uncles who staggered around town in a drunken stupor. My hair and clothes always smelled like cigarettes, because even in the summertime my uncles would smoke inside, but the smell was the worst in the winter when we couldn't even open the windows. The people at church would sneak glances at me and cast their eyes downward, and I'd sit as still as I could and listen to the pastor talk to me about hope and salvation.

If I got there early, sometimes the whole group of church people were standing outside the building waiting to go in, and I couldn't stand having to walk through the group of them, so I'd just go home. But most days, I was able to get through it.

First were the Sunday school lessons at 9:00, then we all got together for "big" church at 10:00. I loved Sunday school and all the Bible stories. I accepted things uncondi- tionally—when the teacher said that Jonah got swallowed by a whale, I knew that Jonah got swallowed by a whale. That one really impressed me; I must have read it a thou- sand times. The story of Jesus broke my heart. This man died on a cross for *me*, just so I could go to heaven?

I felt proud whenever I raised my hand and knew an answer. You'd get gold stars for lots of things, like bringing in your Bible or knowing a verse by heart. They'd put your name up on the board and put gold stars next to your name, and boy, did that matter to me. It was really big. It takes more than that to get kids excited today, but gold stars were the ultimate in coolness to me then.

It all meant something to me, more than I expect it meant to other kids my age. For most of the other kids, death was just a concept. For me, it was a reality that I thought about all the time. My dad died, and my mom died, and when you live with that so young, you feel as if you could die any minute. Life feels really rickety, so you sure do wonder if there's anything afterward. People told me my mom went to heaven when she died, and I wanted to be with her, so I paid attention in church when they told me you have to accept Jesus to go to heaven. *Where do I sign up?*

Later, Bobby and I had a thousand conversations where we tried to tell ourselves that our mom would have done the right thing at the end. Had she asked for forgiveness? Jesus would have given it in a second if she had asked, and if only we knew, we could feel so much safer knowing that she was in heaven.

The death of my mom affected me pretty deeply emotionally and physically. I was always having stomach aches and headaches. Even though we didn't have the money, my grandmother took me to the doctor often. One of those, in the waiting room, had Bible storybooks, and at the back of the books there were these cards that said, "If you're interested in having somebody show you the entire group of these Bible storybooks, please fill this out." So I filled it out. No postage was required!

Into my grandmother's mailbox it went, and I put the flag up. About a month later, this Asian man came up to the door and he says he's here to sell the Bible books that we inquired about. He had this big suitcase. My grandmother said, "I don't know what you're talking about," and he pulled out the slip that I filled out while I tried to look real innocent. I got in such trouble for that! We couldn't even afford a phone, and I was thinking we're getting a whole series of Bible books.

I could still look at them at church, though. I treasured the books, all full of pictures and stories I could read. In the drawings, Jesus looked just like my uncle RJ—which I told my grandma all the time. "Don't you think RJ looks like Jesus?" She laughed, but I was pretty convinced that there was something to it. Sometimes I felt like RJ *was* Jesus, sitting there in my house in the midst of all this craziness. There was a peace that always surrounded him.

Meanwhile, our home was quickly becoming a Motel 6. Grandma took in stray family members like stray dogs. Whenever someone got divorced, or got evicted, or whatever, we'd wind up with new houseguests. There were just four rooms, so most people wound up sleeping in the living room. Bobby never even had a room, just a couch.

I hated it. I hated that there were always people sharing our groceries and using up the hot water, when we didn't have enough money for our own groceries, let alone other people's. And what was even worse was that now there was an audience watching my humiliation. More than the physical, more than the sexual, the verbal abuse is what bothered me most. It was a constant backdrop in my life, just an endless stream of taunts about how my parents were awful and I was worthless and my grandma didn't really want me and I'd never amount to anything. It felt worse when they did it in front of people.

The pastor and the Sunday school teachers didn't seem to agree with my uncles, though. They talked about Jesus, who loved everybody, and who had plans for people. I felt sure He had a plan for me.

One Sunday, the pastor took an altar call. "Do you want to make Jesus your personal Lord and Savior?"

For the first time I can remember, God spoke to me and said, "Do it."

I knew I had to. I had to walk past all those important people and their well-dressed kids and go up to the altar to make Jesus my Lord. Every week, I wore the same pink dress and the only shoes I owned—brown clogs. *I* knew it looked horrible and *they* knew it looked horrible, but I didn't care. I decided that day to walk down the aisle. One step, two steps . . . that little walk from the back of the church to the front felt so long, and the whole way I could hear people whispering, "That's the little girl from the Projects. That's the one whose parents were alcoholics . . ."

When I got to the altar, the pastor said, "Do realize what you've done? Do you understand?" I said, "Absolutely."

Afterwards, people came up to me and said congratulations, and the pastor said the decision I made that day was going to affect where I spent the rest of eternity. I knew he was right. I didn't do it because it was a fad and all the other kids were getting saved. I did it because I was convicted. I knew that God is who He says He is.

That day when I went home, I had a secret. I knew that I had a best friend who would be with me all the time, and when my uncles would yell and cuss, I had this friend nobody knew about who would tell me it was okay. Me and my friend Jesus would share jokes about how stupid my uncles were. To this day, I think the only reason I didn't develop multiple personalities was that Jesus was always there talking in my ear. When my uncles told me I was a piece of trash, Jesus told me I was *somebody*.

From then on, I was in church every time the doors were open. I sang off-key in the choir, I performed in every play, and I had season tickets to the back row of every sermon. The important people may have looked down on me, but I could either be mocked at church or abused at home. I wasn't crazy—I picked church!

When I prayed I would tell God how mad I was that my mom couldn't live for me. How tired I was of getting screamed at and called horrible names. How I wanted my uncles to die for the way they treated my grandmother and me. He understood me, and it was always okay to talk to Him to get those feelings out. He even thought my brown clogs and my big ole' cowlick were pretty.

The devil got what he wanted from my mother. He wasn't going to win with me.

Sometimes I brought Karen with me to church, but most of the time I went alone. My grandma wouldn't go there. She didn't feel right among the "rich" people. It's funny when I think about it now, because I know now that most of them weren't really rich—but just about everyone seemed rich to us back then. Sometimes people in small towns who have a little success think they're bigger than they are.

When my uncles were sober, they would almost seem nice. And when they weren't, they would taunt me about going to church, just like they taunted me about everything. "You're a hypocrite like all those other fake people at that church," they'd say. On the ride to the church, I would feel horribly guilty about leaving my grandmother with them. Who knew what they would say or do to her while I was gone? What a traitor I was, having a respite when she was stuck with those jerks. But she wouldn't come with me.

At home, I always wanted to be the center of attention— at least, her attention. I watched every beauty pageant on television and wanted to be a star just like Miss America or Miss USA. I told her I was going to be famous someday, which of course meant that I needed to start practicing immediately. I'd stand in front of the television and sing and dance, or make up skits and perform them by myself or with Karen.

Grandma might be watching the news or *Sanford & Sons*, and I'd just get up right in front of the television and launch into a show tune. If I needed a better excuse for attention, I would practice my "presentations" for Girl Scouts or my church group, Girls in Action.

"Tracy, I just want to watch this one show," she'd say.

"But I need to practice in front of an audience!"

Her head would tilt over during my presentation, and I'd get irritated.

"Grandma, wake up!"

"Grandma's not asleep, Tracy. She's just resting her eyes."

"Well, you look asleep."

Then I'd make her sit up and pay better attention. How was I ever going to be a star if I couldn't get my own grandma to stay awake through my brilliant performances?

She wasn't thinking about stardom, though. She was just trying to get by. By all means, she was a survivor. When we had nothing but potatoes to eat, she would find a way to make ten different dishes with potatoes, and they would all be good. Her potato soup was the best thing on Earth.

We walked to the bank one day together and she asked for a loan. I'm not sure what it was for, but the banker told her no, and she cried. Cried. Begged him, but he still said no. It was a long walk home. Obviously, whatever she needed the money for wasn't going to happen, and my uncles would find a way to make that my fault somehow. Like if only I hadn't been there to be a burden on my grandma, they would all be eating caviar and living the good life.

I would know in my gut what kind of day it was going to be the instant I stepped onto the sidewalk that led to the front door of my house. I could just tell whether my uncles were drunk or sober. If they were drunk, it was going to be a very, very bad day. If they were sober, it would be okay.

What we did at the house and how I acted around my uncles changed depending on whether they were drunk or sober. On their sober days, I would roll cigarettes for them. They'd buy Prince Albert tobacco in a can and show me how to roll the paper around the loose tobacco. This started when I was maybe seven years old . . . it's funny, but I loved doing it. One of my uncles made a poor man's Slip 'n' Slide for me and Karen in the backyard, and we'd get in our bathing suits and play around with no worry or self-consciousness at all. I wouldn't do that if they were drunk. I wouldn't wear a bathing suit in front of them, and I wouldn't want Karen to, either.

It was like they were completely different people. I made almost no association between the drunk uncles and the sober uncles. Sure, they looked alike, but that's where the similarities ended.

I remember the anxiety I would feel whenever they were sober and about to leave the house. My stomach would twist and turn. I just knew everything was about to be ruined.

"Please don't go out drinking," I would say.

"I'm not going to get drunk," Len would say. "I'm just going to the store. Why do you worry so much?"

Then he would come home as his alter ego, the drunken jerk, and my heart would break.

They all knew it was wrong, because they tried to quit every few months. One of my uncles who didn't usually live with us got sober for at least two years, and it was devastating the day he showed up on our door smelling of alcohol. I remember thinking this was what it meant to "fall off the wagon." He sure was in the right place to relapse, though; my uncles were happy to help him get as loaded as possible.

Somehow they managed to pull it together decently for holidays, most of the time. Mother's Day, Easter, Christmas . . . when company was coming, my grandma would tell them, "I don't want all of you going out and getting drunk and embarrassing me." Maybe they figured they had a reputation to uphold, so they usually dialed down the meanness at family gatherings. They usually didn't curse out my aunts or get into physical fights with each other. But they were still insulting to me and my brothers and still inappropriate in front of people. I used to think, *These people know I have to stay here after they leave. They know I'm here with three grown drunk men tonight.*

When I think back on it, I wonder how none of them ever knew what was going on. I can't believe that they never thought anything of the way Len would always pull on me and pretend to hug me. All the while he was rubbing my chest. He would always try to pull me on his lap, tickle me, or grab me between the legs. If I encountered that as an adult I would find it very odd. I would not think it "all right" for a drunk man to have his hands all over a child. Maybe they all believed it was an accident, that he couldn't *really* mean to touch me like that. I have to hope that's what they believed, because it's hard to accept—the alternative—that they knew and just didn't care. I guess it's easier to pretend you just didn't see something than to deal with what you saw.

One of my cousins did make an effort once to get me out of there. He was a good man, had good jobs and nice cars, and was a cultured person. I had just come home from school, and I remember him showing up and talking to my grandma.

"We found a house trailer for you and Tracy," he said. "We can put it on my land and you can come live with me. I found a school for Tracy, and it's real nice . . ."

He was so nervous, you could tell. And it turned out he had good reason to be nervous, because my grandma threw a fit. She freaked out and walked out of the house and down the street to her sister's house and wouldn't speak to my cousin for some time after that.

My cousin was heartbroken because he was trying to do a good thing, and I thought it sounded like a great idea, but like everything else in life, Grandma couldn't see past her "boys." What would happen to her boys? She couldn't leave them! How dare anyone suggest such a thing?

So no one ever did again. Everyone just pretended that it was okay to live the way we did.

Walking by Len's room down the hallway gave me the creepy feeling as if you've seen something you're not sup- posed to see. He would watch porn movies in his room all the time with the door wide open, masturbating on his bed. You could hear all the noises, and it made me sick. Everything about that room was demonic and disgusting. It smelled like cigarettes and vomit and body odor.

He would make me come into his room and watch movies with him. They weren't what we'd call porn today—at least not "hard-core" porn—but they were completely inappropriate for kids, and always with sexual overtones. The one that replays in hazy skips in my mind is *Cat People*, which is described as "erotic horror," but if you want to be real about it, it's soft-core porn about an incestuous relationship.

I was twelve when the movie came out, and I just don't have the nerve to watch it again now, but it doesn't surprise me that this is the one that I remember best. A man who fantasizes about having sex with his younger family member? Yes, it's too close for comfort. I couldn't believe he wanted me to watch it.

Not that it should have surprised me. I used to lock the door to my bedroom at night, and Len would shake the handle and yell at me. "I don't know why you lock your door. Nobody wants to bother you! Nobody wants to come in here and see you! You're always thinking someone wants to bother you."

Sure, I thought. *So why are you trying to unlock my door if no one wants to come in and bother me? Get away from my door!*

He never came into the bedroom where me and my grandma were sleeping. I guess there were some lines even he wouldn't cross . . . but not many. Len would buy *Playboy* magazines and leave them out, just to "catch" me looking at them.

"You like looking at that stuff," he said. "That's what you like."

I remember feeling so guilty just for seeing the covers of those magazines. He tried to make me feel like I was bringing it on myself, that I was perverted, that it was my fault. I knew it wasn't my fault, but I didn't know whose fault it was. I blamed my mom and dad for dying and for leaving me in this house. I blamed all my relatives who pretended not to see when he touched me inappropriately. I blamed my grandma for choosing them over us.

Mostly, I just tried not to make waves. I would tell Len that I didn't like it, that I didn't want to watch those movies with him because they were "gross," but a lot of the time, I just had to appease the drunk person. My pre-teen years were all about walking on eggshells, trying to blend in with the walls, hoping he wouldn't see me.

"Come in here," he'd say. "I want to show you something about this movie." That's how it would start. You don't know what it is when you're that young, but now I know what those stains on his sheets were. Now I know what he was doing right next to me. He made me watch him sometimes.

There weren't a lot of words exchanged in his room. I had nothing to say, really, and he would just talk drunken nonsense. Things that didn't even pertain to me. He'd just rant about how he was sick of everybody and cuss a lot. I think he did that just to pretend that what was happening wasn't happening. I imagine that if you want someone to watch you pleasure yourself, you don't want to admit that's what you're doing.

And I did what he told me to, because in my mind it was better than a fight. It was better than him yelling at me and calling me the things he did. So I just tried to be invisible when I walked past his room, real fast, heart pounding. It didn't happen every day, but it happened a lot, from when I was seven to when I was about fourteen.

When I was little, he threatened me that I would get kicked out of the house and live in an orphanage if I told on him. "Who will believe you?" he would ask. At the time his advances started, I didn't even know what it all meant. I was too innocent to understand what he was doing. As I got older, I knew it was dysfunctional and wrong, but what choice did I have? I felt like I needed to just keep it together and not complain because I was lucky to be there and have a place to stay. Maybe this was just the price I had to pay. Some days I couldn't see past the next day, and sometimes I could see twenty years into my future—it depended on the day. This whole thing felt like a bad dream, and when I got angry about it, I mostly thought about my mom. If only she wouldn't have been an alcoholic, none of this would have happened.

Sometimes I would overhear people in my family saying, "It's so sad the way she just died when he died," and I would think, "What was so great about him? What's wrong with me? Why did she love him so much and not us?"

The "what ifs" went through my mind a lot, and I kept asking myself how I got there and what I did wrong. At the ripe old age of eight or nine, what had I done to deserve all this?

Why can't you bring her back? I'd ask Jesus. *Bring her back, only this time, make her not be sick. Bring her back, but I want her back without the drinking.*

Much as I loved my grandmother, she wasn't my mother. And I couldn't tell her about this.

I often wonder now what would have happened if I told her what Len was doing to me. She was so protective of them, so insistent that they were called to act the way they did, like they suffered from a condition they couldn't possibly help. Knowing that sealed my mouth shut, because I don't think she would have believed me. Somehow, it would have been my fault. And I don't think I could have taken that. At that point, I would rather suffer through what I was going through alone than have to start hating her for telling me it was my fault.

When you have a favorite celebrity, sometimes it's better not to meet them or read too much about them, because it can ruin the image you have of them. That's how it was with her. Had she not taken up for me, it would have ruined the image I had of her, and I guess I just couldn't find that out. I already knew that she wouldn't kick them out—she'd told us that clearly enough time and again—so I preferred to comfort myself by believing that she was oblivious. Then I could still pretend that she would have picked me, just this once, if only she knew.

But history had shown that to be rather unlikely.

One summer day, Karen, my grandma, and I were shelling peas on the porch when Bobby came home from work. He was doing construction work on homes that summer and was about to sit down next to us and take his boots off, but uncle Ronald came outside and began taunting him.

"You sorry fool and your sorry job," he said, slithering out onto the porch.

"Ronald, I don't want to bother with you today," Bobby said. "I'm tired. Get away from me."

"Make me."

"That's enough. Leave him alone," my grandmother said.

"Shut up, you stupid old bitch," said Ronald.

Right then, I knew it was about to be *on*. Bobby just couldn't let things like that go. Maybe if Ronald had just stuck to cussing at him, it would have been dropped, but you just couldn't disrespect women—especially Grandma or our mom or me—around Bobby. It set off a fire in him . . . and of course, our uncles knew that very well.

I felt Bobby tensing up. Calmly, he turned to me and said, "Tracy, move."

I did, and he grabbed Ronald and rammed his face straight into the huge pine tree in our front yard. By the end of their fight, Ronald was lying on the ground, and Bobby just kept kicking him with his steel-toed construction boots. The crazy thing was that Ronald was still mouthing off, even while Bobby was kicking him in the face!

My grandma was hysterical, wringing her hands and yelling at Bobby to stop. But I didn't want him to stop. *Keep on!* I thought. *Get him good!* Sure enough, as usual, my grandma walked next door and called the police to take Bobby away.

Soon as Bobby realized that's what happened, he turned and said, "Tracy, you want to come with me?"

We left Ronald lying there bleeding, and we walked to a diner where we ordered cheeseburgers and played pool for a while, figuring that the police wouldn't stay long.

That's why I couldn't tell Bobby about what Len was doing to me, though. If he would get into such a bloody fight over my uncle's mouthing off, I knew what would have happened if I told him how bad things really were. He would have killed Len and gone to prison, and I never would have seen my brother again.

"Your grandma," Bobby would say. "I don't know why she has to call the police on me all the time."

"She's not just *my* grandma, she's yours, too," I'd say. "And I don't know why she does it, either. You were defending her."

"Yeah, she's my grandma. But Ronald's her *baby*."

We were used to this by now. When the uncles fought with my brothers, my grandma would try to break it up. If she couldn't get it broken up, I would run across the yard to the neighbor's house to call the police, because we didn't have our own phone. It wasn't a long run, but it felt like it took forever because I knew that if my uncles caught me out there, I'd get it.

When the police got there, my grandma would always point the finger of blame at Bobby and tell them to arrest him. "These kids start with me, and I have to put them in their place," my uncle would explain. Grandma was the ultimate enabler. Off Bobby would go in the police car, and every time, his spirit broke a little more. My uncles would cackle with laughter as they watched the car drive off with Bobby in the back seat, and I would want God to strike them down right there to make them stop laughing.

What my grandmother didn't know is that the police would just drive around the corner and let Bobby out, saying, "I'm so sorry you have to live this way."

The fact that he got into trouble probably isn't surprising. But the funny thing is that even though he didn't go to church, he would give me wads of cash to give to the church, from the money he made working construction jobs or doing whatever he could find to do. He was basically tithing, but he didn't know what that was at the time.

"Here, put this in the collection plate at your Sunday school," he'd tell me, and thrust three hundred dollars in my hands. That's a lot of money now, but it was *really* a lot of money then.

My grandma would pull me aside and say, "Don't give

that all to the church. Keep some of that cash because Bobby's going to need it later."

She was right. I would keep half of it and hide it from him some weeks, and when he was broke later, I'd give it back, or we'd use it to buy groceries. After a while, he knew what was going on, and he'd ask my grandma, "What happened to the money that Tracy stole from the church?" She would tell him, "You're eating the money!" We would tease her sometimes about stealing the church money, and that would make her so mad. She'd say, "They get enough money."

But I always gave the other half of his money to the church like he said to do. I'd come walking up with my little purse filled with cash, and I'm sure the church ladies wondered, "What in the world is up with this child?" I still wasn't in the front row, but I sure looked important when that collection plate came around.

Soon, Bobby got sent to jail for DUI. In those days, you actually went to a prison work camp for things like that—they didn't mess around. So I lost my protector for six months.

The police still visited us regularly. I would take that scary run in the dark over to the neighbor's house to make the call when things got really out of hand; sometimes my grandma would tell me to call, and sometimes it was my own decision to do it. Out the back door I went, holding the door handle to make sure it closed slowly and quietly— if it slammed shut, they'd hear and I'd be in major trouble. Then I'd do the speed-walking thing. *Please hear me and wake up*, I'd pray as I knocked on the door. *Don't let me risk this for nothing.*

It could be two or three in the morning, but our neighbor would let me in. I'd stay at her place until the police arrived, so I didn't have to worry about what my uncles would do to me in between.

When the officers showed up, one of them would say to my grandma, "Do you want us to take them to jail and keep them for a couple of days to sober up and give you a break?"

"I don't know," she'd say to them. "If they settle down, they can stay here, but they need to know that they have to settle down. Tell them to quit fighting so me and Tracy can get some sleep. Tracy has school tomorrow, and it's late and they're upsetting her."

I'd look at her like she was crazy. *Woman, I just poked a tiger with a stick and you think they're just going to settle down?*

But she was serious. She just wanted the police to tell them to hush; she wouldn't let them actually do anything. I'm not sure why they never took me away. Maybe Child Protective Services wasn't as strict back then. Maybe they just figured I loved her so much that it was better to leave me with her than get moved to a foster home somewhere. Again, I just chose to believe that they didn't know how bad things were or what would happen when they left.

Every now and then I got lucky and they'd be close enough to passing out that they would just go to bed, but normally, they stayed awake to taunt me. I'd run to grandma's room and lock the door, and I'd lie there in bed with my eyes wide in panic as they yelled out.

"Don't you ever call the police again, you little whore! I'm your boss. I tell you what to do. I will whip you. This is my momma's house, and they're not going to take me to jail. You watch it, you little jerk. They aren't gonna do anything to me. They know better. It's *my house!*"

Maybe it is, I thought. After all, they were still out in the living room, and nothing ever happened to them. Maybe the police couldn't do anything to them no matter what they did, because the house was part-theirs if their mother paid the rent. That part was never very clear to me. All I knew is that it seemed they had special exemption from all the rules other people needed to live by.

"You just act like you don't hear them and go to sleep," my grandma would say.

Some days I knew it was never going to change. I was going to be tormented by these fools forever.

Over the summers, I spent weeks with one of my cousins. My grandma would put me on the bus with my little blue suitcase, and I'd sit right behind the bus driver. His name was Slim and he was ten feet tall. We stopped in every town to pick people up, and I would chatter away excitedly the whole ride. Once I got there, I knew I'd get to play and bake and forget my uncles for a while.

We were usually together on Easter, and I'd get an Easter basket and a dress. Once I got a cupcake with a chick on it, and when I would get upset about the way things were in my life, I would think of that a lot. When you don't have many happy memories, it makes the ones you do have seem bigger and more important, so the cupcake took on a lot of meaning. Spending time in a house where I was safe was a huge treat.

The trips home from my cousins house were very different. Slim would know that I didn't feel like talking.

"Tracy, why are you always so quiet on the way home?" he asked.

"My stomach hurts."

"Why does your stomach hurt on the way home all the time? There's no reason for your stomach to hurt . . ."

I knew what he meant. But there was nothing to say, really. I told him that I had fun with my cousin, but I missed my grandma, too. And I just sat there and tried not to feel sick, tried to prepare myself for what was coming.

Maybe RJ missed me, I thought. So I'd visit him when I got home and tell him all about my summer adventures with Sandra.

"Where are you going?" Ronald would ask.

"I'm going to see RJ," I'd say.

"He doesn't want you bothering him. Why do you think he wants to listen to a stupid kid like you?" he would say, and if RJ heard that, he would come out and get me and bring me to his room. *Ha!*

RJ never came out of his room when we had family over, so I brought his food in to him.

"I know you don't want to go out there," I said. "I'll sit here with you."

He would motion to the door, as if to say, "I'm fine. Go ahead."

"No, it's okay. I'd rather be with you than them." That would make him smile.

Then one morning, I went with Karen into RJ's room to wake him up, and he didn't move. I shook him, but he wouldn't wake up. He looked just like he always did when he slept: hands on his chest, in his white shirt and pants on top of the covers.

You've got to be kidding me, I thought.

My last security blanket, gone. The only uncle I *didn't* want to die. He died in his sleep, and I never knew why. It was just one of those things.

When we cleaned out his closet after he died, there were papers from the floor to the ceiling. Just a few pairs of pants and shirts and one pair of shoes, and the whole rest of the closet was stacks of paper. Finally, we'd see what he was writing all that time with his pencils and loose-leaf paper.

Over and over and over, RJ had been writing one thing: The Bible.

— *Four* —

I DON'T THINK THERE WAS EVER A PARTICULAR moment when I said, "I'm not going to take this anymore," but when I was about fourteen years old, Len stopped sexually abusing me. Slowly, I had been changing into a teenager, and shedding my childhood fears and submissiveness. When he tried to touch me inappropriately, I would pull away or tell him to stop. I didn't feel the need to please so much anymore, and I was learning to stand up to my uncles.

Well, at least I was learning to mouth off better. My whispered "shut up"s became louder. They would call me names no child should ever hear, and I would say, "Who are you to call me names?" Whenever I talked back to them, my grandmother would give me a hard time, though, which was embarrassing. Half the time, I was standing up for her—someone I loved more than life—and she would make me feel like I was doing something wrong to insult her precious children.

When I was younger, they would push me and jerk my arm and grab me and yell in my face, "Look at me!" I didn't know that was abuse, because they never flat out punched me. And if I got tangled up in their fights with each other and I got hit, well, that was just an accident and I shouldn't have gotten in the way. Grandma would yell at me not to get in the middle of them, but really, was it my fault for trying to stop them, or theirs for not having the sense to stop swinging when a child was in-between them?

My definition of abuse was pretty narrow. I knew Karen's mom was abusing her because I saw her get hit in the face, but I didn't realize that all the pushing and grabbing and fondling and porn movies were abuse. I knew it was wrong, but I didn't know it was abuse.

As I entered my teenage years, I wasn't easy to mess with anymore. I was more confident, stronger physically and emotionally. *To hell with him. To hell with everybody here*, I thought. I didn't need to try to keep peace with everyone anymore; I realized it wasn't my job. And I think that's what scared Len. Toward the end, I think he was afraid that I was going to tell someone. He knew I wasn't easy to silence anymore.

But I never did. I told him, "You make me sick." That was my favorite line. But I never told my grandma, or my brothers, or my aunts, or my pastor, or my teachers, or anyone, about what he did to me. I was always afraid it would be turned around on me, that people wouldn't believe me, or that my grandma wouldn't take up for me.

Instead, I followed in Bobby's footsteps and just tried to have a life of my own and stayed out of the house as much as I could. I joined all the church activities and the cheerleading squad and entered beauty pageants. I had lots of friends from school. I wouldn't invite them over to my house, mostly because I was afraid that my uncle Len would touch all the girls inappropriately or that all my uncles would say horrible things to me in front of them. I really didn't need them all hearing my uncles call me a whore.

My uncles sometimes tried to make me feel guilty for my after-school activities. Every day after cheerleading practice, I would use my grandmother's grocery account to buy a Coke and snacks, and she had to buy my uniform and all my school supplies. One of my uncles, in particular, would make comments about how I was costing my grandma so much money. But the thing was, she got all my Social Security checks and used them for the whole household. *If they didn't live with us*, I thought, *my grandma and I could get along just fine on those checks. We could move to a smaller place and use fewer groceries. It isn't my responsibility to support them.* Sometimes I had to remind myself of that when the guilt sneaked in.

In no way was I a frivolous kid, but I just wanted to be allowed to buy a Coke and be a normal high school girl sometimes, not a charity case. My grandma made a lot of my clothes on her sewing machine. I remember when the button-down Oxford shirts with the big collars were "in," and my grandma sewed me a yellow one that was pretty hideous. It was embarrassing, but I wore it so I wouldn't break her heart. Most of my other clothes were hand-me-downs that other parents gave us. When other kids know you're wearing their clothes, it's pretty humiliating, but I was still popular. The teachers liked me and the students liked me, and I was always on the homecoming court.

Grandma was old-fashioned about me wearing makeup or bras, and if I wore anything form-fitting, she would tell me it was inappropriate. But she still let me play beauty shop with her, just around the house. I always wanted to fix her hair and makeup, and by the time I was done with her, she'd look like a clown.

My picture was in the paper every other week because I kept winning beauty pageants. I started entering them after my cousin entered one and told me how much fun it was. The pageants didn't cost us any money because I got sponsors and borrowed dresses. People didn't buy dresses back then; mostly, we all rented dresses, crinoline and all. I never wanted my grandma to come to the pageants. I don't know why, but it made me too nervous—I was afraid to lose in front of her, afraid I'd disappoint her. So I'd have a friend's mom drive me, and then I'd come home with a big trophy and crown to show Grandma, who was always sitting out on the porch waiting for me.

In my early teens, Grandma went with me to one of those expensive country pageant shops where the salespeople can really make you feel like dirt if you don't have any money. There, we found this turquoise dress with sequins and a chiffon skirt, and it was one of those movie-star moments when I put it on.

"That's the dress!" the salesladies all said. And it was. It was the perfect dress for me. But it wasn't for rent.

I don't remember exactly what it cost, but maybe a couple hundred dollars. Enough to make tears form in my grandma's eyes because we couldn't afford it. But I wanted it so much, and it was so beautiful, that we ended up buying it on credit. She made payments of about twenty dollars a month until it was paid off.

When we got home with the dress, my uncles started in.

"Don't tell me you're spending money to buy her that stuff. She doesn't need that fancy stuff, that little spoiled brat!"

"No, we didn't buy it," she lied. "We just rented it."

My heart sunk. I knew it was my money from my dead parents that bought that dress, and I didn't know why she had to lie about it. It was like she was agreeing with them that I wasn't worth the money. I wanted her to say, "She deserves this dress, and it's her money, and she looks beautiful in it. And it's none of your business anyway!"

Why couldn't she have stood up for me just once like that?

But I rationalized that if she told them we bought it, they just would have tried to tear it up or ruin it. They'd want to teach me a lesson. But if they thought it was rented, they wouldn't ruin it or we wouldn't get our money back.

I wore the dress to at least four or five pageants, and I still loved it. What I enjoyed so much about these pageants was that I could live in this fantasy world where I had beautiful dresses and felt like a little lady, and no one knew about what was going on at my house. It gave me something to be proud of. There was always a twinge of sadness mixed in, though, because I would see all the girls with their parents getting ready. Their moms would fix their hair and fuss with their dresses, but I didn't have family there. Sometimes I'd catch a ride with my aunt if my cousin was competing, too, but mostly I got rides from the other kids' parents.

My third-grade teacher showed up at one of my pageants when I was about sixteen. I think she always kept a special place for me in her heart. I remember that she would come to school with her hair wet, smelling like a perm. On some weekends, I rode my bike to her house. She was in her early twenties when she started teaching, and one day she told us that we were going to have a new teacher named Mrs. Cronwell on Monday. I think I cried. Then on Monday, she was back—she had gotten married over the weekend, so she had a new last name. She was Mrs. Cronwell. What a relief!

Even after I was out of her class, she'd come pick me up in her hatchback and tell me to bring my pillow and blanket so I could sleep in the car, and we'd listen to Jim Croce all the way to her parents' house about an hour and a half away. She would let Karen come with us, too. I didn't know why she was that way with us, but I suspect she might have known what it was like to live with alcoholics.

All the time, she'd tell me how smart I was and how good I was. I didn't tell her about the things my uncles said and did to me because I didn't want to ruin her image of me. "Oh, I just felt like saying hi," I'd tell her when I rode my bike to her place. But she and her new husband knew, I'm sure. Little girls don't just go visiting adults to say hi if everything's okay at home.

We didn't know what to say to each other when I saw her at the pageant. She had seen me in the paper, and I guess she wanted to see what became of that sad little girl. It meant a lot to me to see her there, even if we didn't know what to talk about. She was always so good to me, even after she wasn't my teacher anymore. All of my teachers were very special to me.

I wasn't always the best student. I loved to read, and I got good grades until the last year or two of high school, but I might have sandbagged a little . . . I didn't want people to know I was really smart, or they'd expect more of me! Teachers were important to me, though, and I was respectful of them. I still go back to visit my old school when I'm in town. There wasn't a lot of normalcy in my life in those years, so my school teachers were about the best role models I had. I liked the discipline they provided.

Some kids thought one of my favorite teachers was too strict, but I defended her. I knew "mean," and she wasn't mean. She was strict for a good cause. She wanted us to do the best we could, and I liked that. So the kids called me the "teacher's pet."

There were seventy-five people in my grade. We all went to school together from kindergarten through twelfth grade, so we knew each other and our families knew each other very well. My grandma trusted me and my friends, and she never gave me a curfew. She said, "You come home when you think you need to be home." So I was always home at ten o'clock. I was never wild. I never slept around, or even kissed boys. I remember confiding in my grandma in about the ninth or tenth grade that the boys didn't pay attention to me. I was too skinny, not curvy like the other girls. It seemed like all the other girls had boyfriends.

"The boys are going to get tired of looking at those girls. When they're done with the other girls, it's you they'll want the most," my grandma told me. Even though I was going through an awkward stage at the time, she made me feel pretty.

Although I did have my own bedroom by then, in my early high school years, I still shared my grandma's room most nights because I felt safer with her. Well, I got it in my head to sneak out one night. My girlfriend and I were going to drive around town with these two boys, football players. I don't know what we were going to do, but I crawled out the window and they picked me up and we made it about a block down the street before I started sobbing.

"What are you doing?" my friend asked, jabbing me.

I said, "What if she has a heart attack? What if something happens to her, and I'm not there?"

Grandma almost never talked about things like that, about the idea that she would die one day, and I tried not to think about it. A couple of times she had told me that she wanted me to have the old wooden china cabinet "if anything happens to me," and I would just say, "Nothing's going to happen to you!" But of course, I was not stupid. One day, she would be gone, and that terrified me.

The football players took me back home. I could've gone in the front door—it was never locked—but I crawled back into the window and back into bed with my grandma, and she knew, and I knew she knew.

That was the start of my youthful experimentation.

When I was about sixteen, I started drinking wine coolers, like all the other kids who got into trucks and drove down the same strip in town, where there was one traffic light. I didn't make the association between my wine coolers and the stuff my uncles drank out of paper bags. To me, it was something social and fun, and I liked the way it felt. It gave me the nerve to say things I never said freely before. It wasn't anything ugly like what my uncles did.

Grandma used a clothes hamper as a night stand, and she had her clock on it. As I got older, I'd stay out later and think I was very clever when I changed her clock backward, then woke her up to say, "I'm home."

One day when my uncle was sober, he said, "You know, Tracy, last night you came home at 11:00 and set the clock back to 10:00. But your grandma didn't go to bed until 10:45." She never said anything about it. For at least a year, I had been messing with the clock, and she let me think I was so smart.

When I had gotten a part-time job, one Mother's Day I decided to buy grandma something special. I had never given her anything very nice. I made her cards out of huge poster board every Mother's Day, and I always bought small gifts from the local drug store for Christmas. But I wanted this to be something truly great to show her how wonderful I thought she was. I was tired of seeing her in dresses all the time, especially her old cotton frocks that dangled over her house shoes. So I bought her a classy pant suit from the local department store. She could wear this to special places like church, or a wedding.

Imagine my disappointment when she returned it. She thanked me, but told me that she would never wear pants. It just wasn't her style. She liked her frocks just fine. Today I might understand that she was just stuck in her ways, but when I was a teenager it frustrated me so badly that she wouldn't let me update her style. Those old frocks are more endearing to me today. So are the home-made cards. When my grandma died, we found all the cards that I ever made in her closet with her frocks and house shoes.

Bobby went through a big transformation around that time. He decided one day that he was never going to let my uncles get to him again, and it was amazing how well he stuck to that. He never again got into a physical fight with them, no matter how they provoked him. He would just sit there at the dinner table and let them yell in his ears and mess with him. They were always testing, testing to see how much it would take to make him lose his cool, but it didn't work.

He had given his heart over to the Lord, and he was going to a Pentecostal church regularly. Then he married the daughter of the town judge and they moved away, but he still visited, and I spent weekends over there sometimes. Bobby didn't like to visit much, because of my uncles. Sometimes he would say that to my grandma, too—"Do you see why I can't come here more often? You're letting them make it so I can't even come over to spend time with you."

I'm sure that was their plan, to make him feel like never visiting. I didn't even want to visit, either, but I was still stuck living there. Or was I?

Bobby and his wife would take me in. I knew they would. They were going to be a lot stricter than my grandma was, and my brother would tell me I was going to hell for wearing a cheerleading skirt, but still . . . I could stay there if I wanted to.

Because he was very devout in his beliefs it was hard to be a teenager around him. When I spent weekends at their house, my sister-in-law would have to sneak my cheerleading uniform out of the house so I could go to the football game. When he found out, she would take the heat for it. But she wanted me to live the way I wanted. Even though I didn't always like his strictness, I was proud of my brother for the way he turned his life around.

One morning, I skipped school and went to visit my friend Josephine at the diner where she worked, waiting tables. I never skipped school, but I was just at the end of my rope that day and needed someone to talk to. My uncles were on another bender, and I felt like I'd lose my mind. She was older than me and good to talk to when I needed it.

I told Josephine about my uncles—some of it, at least.

"Tracy, do they ever touch you?" she asked, and I said no because I didn't want to say yes.

And then the Challenger exploded.

The television was on in the diner, and everyone gasped in unison as we all watched it replay over and over, that terrible moment when the space shuttle broke apart seventy-three seconds into flight, killing all seven astronauts. It was something about that teacher, Christa McAuliffe, that made it feel even more tragic. I sat there watching that television and feeling like my whole world had gone crazy, like this was the beginning of the end . . . and in some dangerous place in my mind, I wished I could trade places with Christa.

At least it was quick, I thought. Not the way I was dying, by slowly rotting from the inside out. I was sixteen, and starting to wonder if my life was worth it anymore. Maybe this was the rapture. Bobby was always talking about the rapture, when Jesus was coming to take his followers to heaven and leave the sinners behind to spend eternity in hell. His rules in his church were a lot different from what I felt Jesus was telling me. Bobby thought that I might get left behind because I wore lipstick. Jesus never told me that my salvation had anything to do with my makeup bag, though.

Maybe those astronauts were the first to go. I sat there brooding and feeling like the world had spun out of control and waiting to see if the sky was about to open up and people were going to go flying off to heaven. I remember that January day as the day I'd had enough. If I didn't change something in my life, I was going to go crazy.

"I want to stay here with you," I told my grandma, "But I can't stay here with you. Not if they're here." It was an ultimatum, really. And she chose them. No matter what, she was never going to kick them out. Not even if it meant I had to leave. "One day, you'll understand," she repeated, and all I could think was, *Woman, get it together. I will never understand this.*

I packed my clothes, and my uncles followed me around tormenting me.

"You're going to leave her here, after all she's done for you? You've done nothing but use her."

It was amazing. They found a way to make me feel terrible for being there and a way to make me feel terrible for not being there. This time they hit a nerve: They wanted me to feel that I was abandoning my grandma.

"Go ahead," Grandma said. "Don't listen to them. Go on over to Bobby's house, and I'll see you in a day or two."

"Yeah, that's fine," Ronald said. "We're better off without you. You're nothing but a damn burden around here anyway. You just leave your poor old grandma here with us."

And that's what drove me crazy. I didn't want to leave my grandma with them. She knew it.

"Tracy, go on. Grandma will be just fine. You know they're not going to hurt me."

I didn't know any such thing. I'd seen them push her down and throw things and break almost everything she owned. What they didn't break, they pawned.

With a heavy and conflicted heart, I got into Bobby's car and drove away. For a while I visited pretty often—but it always got ugly, so I stopped coming around much. So much guilt built up inside me for leaving her. At her eightieth birthday party, I showed up with a girlfriend from school, and I remember how excited she was that I was there. That made me feel even more guilty. She shouldn't have had to look so excited. I should have been there more often.

But she could have made the choice, I reminded myself. *I didn't want to leave her.*

On one of my visits, I was horrified by what I saw. The bathroom was so filthy, and the whole house was nasty. Keep in mind that my grandmother was the kind of woman who ironed underwear. That kind of filth was not normal. As I walked into the kitchen, grandma was there making a hamburger. That was her thing: she made the *best* hamburgers. She started making one for me because she was happy to see me, and it would feel a little bit like old times.

I went to clear a bit of counter space for her, and I picked up a damp, moldy dish towel. Cockroaches scooted out from under it. Right then one of my uncles came in. "This isn't Burger King! She doesn't need to cook for you. You walked out on her!"

Well, that was it. I took the pan of hot grease and threw it at him.

"I'm done," I told my grandma. "I will never come back to this house as long as they're here."

I stormed out furious and sad. I felt bad for not staying with her and not cleaning up the mess I had made; I felt guilty for being disgusted. (To this day I don't use dish towels—just paper towels.) I had cleaned that bathroom so many times and one more time wouldn't have been a big deal. But with my uncle there, I couldn't stay. I had left for good. In June, she called and asked me to stay with her for a couple of weeks because my uncles were out of town working. It was so good just to be together with her again. I lay my head in her lap while she scratched my back, which

I never could do when my uncles were around—they would make nasty comments. We talked about life and boys and school and slept in her room.

Months earlier, I had told her that I had a chance to graduate early from high school. I could have finished at the end of the eleventh grade, which was the year coming up. I was thinking about it, just finishing what I needed to finish and getting a full-time job somewhere. She didn't want me to do it at the time, but now she had changed her mind.

"I think you should graduate early," she said.

"Why?" I asked.

"I would really like to know that if something happens to me, you're going to finish school."

So I promised her I would. It was too late now for me to graduate early, but I told her I was sure she would see me graduate on time. It was the only time I can ever remember her talking about the future and what she wanted from me. I had always told her I wanted to be something great, but I wasn't very boisterous about my big plans because Grandma couldn't see what I saw.

In my hometown, most people born there would stay their whole lives. They would get married, raise their families, and make ends meet without a lot of job opportunities, the best being at the bank, courthouse, or the state prison. If someone got lucky, maybe he or she could become a manager. That would mean success. Lots of people went to college, but they'd come right back home and work these jobs. You're not expected to want anything better or different, or people make fun of you for having pipe dreams.

Plenty of people went to college, and you always heard of someone moving off and having a great career. But those people, for the most part, came from different circumstances than I did, and they had the support of their parents. Staying there and working wasn't bad. I knew of people who were very happy. I just knew I didn't want to be there for the rest of my life.

I never talked about it much at home because I would have been taunted and accused "trying to be uppity." And I knew my grandma would worry not just about me leaving but about me getting harassed by everyone in the house. She didn't like change, and if I left, well, that would be a change. Finishing high school and getting a good paying job, that was enough for her. But not for me.

That's just how I felt. When my grandma worked as a caretaker and I tagged along, I would think, *I don't ever want to be somebody's caretaker.* Instead, I wanted to be the people she was taking care of. They were some of the nicest houses I'd ever seen, filled with all these beautiful cabinets. I equated those cabinets with success. "One day," I had told my grandma, "I'm going to build you a house with cabinets just like the rich people have."

Our poverty never made me think that she was any less of a person, but I wanted more from life than she had. I don't think she could have ever envisioned what I meant by that. You just weren't supposed to entertain such lofty thoughts when you lived in the Projects. You were supposed to hope for something along the lines of Oprah's grandma's "good white folks."

But I was going to leave this little town someday, I knew. My family would make predictions about how I was going to end up, blaming my grandma for letting me "run wild" with too much freedom.

"Tracy's a good girl," she'd tell them. "She's going to be good at whatever she wants to do."

All I could think about was how I wanted life to always be like this, just me and my grandma in her house, talking and cuddling and taking care of each other. It was a good two weeks, and at the end she said to me, "I'm going to make them move out soon and you can come back home."

"I will," I told her. It was just what I had been praying for.

We planned that I would move back in with her when the new school year started. We would get a smaller house to rent in the Projects. My thought process was that if there was room for only the two of us, then my uncles couldn't stay there. I said, "There will be a rule that no one can sleep on the floor or the couch," because we knew that even if the place had just one bedroom, they would try to stay there anyway.

She said she was going to look into the smaller rentals, and I left there feeling so happy. Things were finally going to work out like they were supposed to, and I would be with my grandma again in just a couple of months.

I went back to Bobby's just as my uncles came home from their job and started drinking to make up for lost time. Grandma never quite got around to making them move out.

Not long after that, my grandma got really ill, and her sister picked her up to take her to the hospital. My uncles walked beside her on the way out to the car, and the whole way, they yelled, "You stupid old bitch! Don't come back!"

She got into her sister's car and they drove off. During the ride, she was real quiet and looking out the window, so her sister asked, "What's wrong?"

She started crying and said, "I won't ever come home again."

Bobby and his wife and I went to see her in the hospital on Sunday, and she said to me, "Come lie here with me," so I climbed into the bed with her. My aunt said, "She doesn't need to be in there with you!" My grandma snapped back, "Just hush. We slept like this for years."

Grandma was Primitive Baptist, and Bobby Pentecostal, and they could never agree on anything. Foot washing, no music, speaking in tongues . . . they argued over everything, and Grandma didn't buy into any of his beliefs. But when we got up to leave that day, she said to Bobby, "Pray for me."

"I always pray for you," he said.

"Pray for me like *you* pray, right now," she said.

So he laid hands on her and prayed in tongues, and Bobby and I made it out to the hallway before we fell apart. My sister-in-law, brother, and I walked out to the car together in near silence because nobody knew what to say. We all just cried and walked and felt our hearts breaking wide open. It wasn't going to be long.

I was going to spend the night at the hospital with her Tuesday night, but she died on Monday. No one called to tell us. It was the next morning when one of my cousins, who rarely even saw my grandma, called Bobby's house to let us know. I have never forgiven my family for making us such an afterthought. I was sleeping on the couch when Bobby woke me up to tell me, then he had to get our brother Dave out of the state prison so he could come to the funeral. It was a Jerry Springer show come to life.

"How could you not call me to tell me?" I yelled at my aunt on the phone.

"Don't call screaming at me," she said. "My mother just died."

"So did mine," I said. "*Twice.*"

The preacher from my grandma's church told me he had gone to see her the night she died, and she said, "I'm tired and I'm ready to go. I know Tracy will be all right, and I can go now."

I was in a haze of crazy when I went to my grandma's house right after she died. My uncles were all laid up drunk, and I was livid. At that point none of them scared me. I would beat the tar out of anybody who said one word to me. I marched in there with eyes full of lunacy and I said, "I'm going to stay here, and I'm sleeping in her room," and they were smart enough not to get near me right then. I don't know what I was hoping to feel or find in that bedroom, but I never wanted to forget. I was going to think about her, and how she smelled, and what her eyes looked like, and the way she dragged her feet when she walked, and how I always knew she was coming down the hallway because of those dragging feet, and how I could always fool her into thinking I was going to wake up and get ready for school even when I was going to fall right back asleep the minute she walked out of the room. Her spirit was still in that room, and I was going to be there with her for one more night.

The next day, we went to the funeral home to pick out a casket and a dress. The newspaper tried to put my name and my brothers' names with the other grandkids in my grandma's obituary, but I told them that I expected us to be listed with the children. For ten years, she had been my mother, father, and grandmother all rolled into one, and no one was going to diminish that now.

My uncles came to the funeral drunk. "How could you even come here, knowing that you killed her?" I said, and they didn't get it.

Nobody seemed to blame them, though. They all seemed angry with me instead, like it was somehow my fault that she died because I left. I left her with them. Or maybe that was just my own guilt talking. I couldn't tell where my screwed-up feelings ended and theirs began anymore. They never said it outright to me, but I always felt that they thought I had jumped ship, and I almost wanted them to say it out loud so I could say, "I wasn't jumping ship. I was under that damn ship!"

But there was a giant weight on my shoulders, questioning what would have happened if I had stayed. Would she still have died? Maybe none of us would have been standing around this casket if I had just gritted my teeth and stayed.

After that, my brother decided to move out of state. That's the way he did things—no planning, just one day, "We're moving." With all the things he had to deal with at such an early age, and the way he always had to be responsible for Dave and me, I think it affected the way he took charge of things. I'm sure I could have gone with him if I wanted, but what did I have there? I didn't want to go to go to a new school in the eleventh grade after growing up with these classmates and teachers. He had a wife and daughter, and as much as I loved being with them, I felt as if I'd be in their way. Bobby and I also fought a lot at that time. He wanted the best for me, but I wanted to be sixteen. I wonder if he ever really got to be sixteen.

We had barely left the funeral when I realized I had nothing whatsoever to live for anymore, and nowhere to go. That's when I decided to toss my life in the garbage. *Cover your eyes, Jesus. This ain't gonna be pretty.*

— *Five* —

AND SO I FELL APART. CONFUSED AND LOST, I began to self-destruct. Who did I have to answer to anymore, anyway? My parents and grandparents were all dead, one brother was in prison, and the other was living out of state. I was angry at God. I felt like everyone I had ever loved had been taken from me. I didn't have faith in anything anymore. I felt abandoned and alone.

As the school year started, I moved in with Linda, a thirty-year-old lady I knew from church who worked at the bank. She was recently divorced, and I sometimes babysat her little girl. She said I could stay with her in her nice Tudor home, as long as I paid rent. I managed to do that.

Even though I was sixteen, the woman treated me like a peer. "I can't tell you what to do," she told me. "You're paying rent." I looked older than my age, and I had a fake ID, so I went out to bars with her on weekends. It was never a big deal to get in. This was when I discovered cocaine and started to understand what was so appealing about alcohol. Cocaine made me feel grown up and stronger, and alcohol helped me forget how sad I was.

Linda was an outspoken woman, very tall and pretty, and we had a lot of fun together. I always sort of felt like I was imposing on her, like she was doing me a huge favor that I needed to pay back. I'm not quite sure why I felt that way, because she was getting a free babysitter and someone to share the expenses with, but I did anyway. She was very well-respected in our town, and I felt like she just took me in out of sympathy, and I was tagging along. All the church people who knew her were very nice to me, and I wondered if they would have been so nice if they met me with my grandma.

No matter how nice she was to me, I felt like a charity case. She would buy me presents at Christmas, and I was still never sure if she wanted me around.

I lived there for two years, while I finished high school. Part of the rent money was from my Social Security checks, and for the rest, I worked at a parts warehouse that was a huge company based in our little town. They sold parts all across the country, and I took orders on the phone. I enjoyed it there, and I liked the people I worked with.

I thought, *Really, what's the point in staying in school?* I might as well just drop out and work full-time. Yeah, I had made that promise to my grandma, but part of me thought, *She's dead. She'll never know.*

After so many years of keeping up my grades and being a teacher's pet, I just stopped caring during my junior year. My grades were the last thing on my mind. Everything seemed so pointless with my grandma gone. Who was I achieving for? Who was going to be proud of me? Who was going to care if I misbehaved and acted like an idiot?

For so long, I was careful never to do anything to embarrass my grandma or make her lose respect for me. I had convinced myself that the reason she wouldn't even let me swear, while she let her boys do whatever they wanted, was that she held me to a higher standard. She thought I was better than that, so I tried to *be* better than that. But my personality changed as soon as she died. Nothing mattered anymore.

So I aimed to just have as much fun as I could, and steered as far away from reality as possible. I tried to completely forget everything about my life up to that point. Late at night thoughts of my grandma would creep into my mind, and I'd push the thoughts away. Sometimes I would see my uncles walking around town, and I would just pretend not to see them and walk the other way.

I'd show up to school just for the social aspects of it. Like homecoming. I was *always* on the homecoming court, and I was very proud of that.

Except that year a teacher came to me and said I couldn't be on the homecoming court. There were requirements about how many school credits you needed, and I didn't have enough. I was devastated, which probably sounds silly, but when your whole life is at rock bottom, these little things you look forward to are lifelines to cling to. They had made a mistake, and I had just enough to participate in homecoming anyway.

Watching me fail broke my teachers' hearts, and the principal's, too. They knew how smart I was, and it was killing them to watch me totally give up. I was on the verge of flunking out. But what could they do? They weren't my parents, and the closest thing I had to a parent was a thirty-year-old who got drunk and high with me on the weekends.

That was also the year I got a boyfriend. We fought a lot, but I loved his parents, and they loved me. I think the main reason I fell for him so hard so fast was that I was in love with the whole idea of a real family—one like his. I figured we were going to get married and live happily ever after, of course.

Linda didn't like that my boyfriend and I argued so much. Like sixteen-year-olds can do, we just talked and talked on the phone for hours every night, and we'd argue over most everything. Even though he wanted to date other people, I was *in love* and was convinced we were supposed to be together forever.

So I'd get into fights in school with the girls who went out with him, and I'd get more and more insecure. We became the small town boyfriend and girlfriend who would fight in the middle of store parking lots, hang out the window of cars to flip each other off all around town, and hang up the phone on each other to show we were *really, really mad*. We broke up and made up every couple of days. Footloose stuff. He never hit me or anything, but it got to where I was wanting to die when he threatened to break up with me, things like that.

It's hard to look back at that now and wonder, *what was I thinking?* I was just so desperate for somebody to love me and want to take care of me. I had lots of other guys interested in me by that point. But I didn't want those other guys. I just wanted this one guy, even though he wasn't interested only in me.

Linda didn't know why I bothered with him, and kept trying to fix me up with older guys. I think she convinced herself that I *was* her peer at some point, so it would be okay to do things together that you're not supposed to do with teenagers.

You know how I said my mom was a sad drunk. I wasn't. I never cried a lot when I was drunk or high; I just got aggressive. And the thing is, I liked it. This angry side of me liked being allowed to come out and act badly.

Despite all the drama and my frequent drinking, I managed to bring my grades up a bit in the twelfth grade, got voted Homecoming Queen, and my boyfriend and I won "Most Popular." Everyone talked about going off to college and all their plans for the future, and they were so excited, but for me it was just scary. School had been the one constant in my life for the past twelve years. Even when my mom died and my grandma died and everything else was upside-down, I still always had school to go to and the same group of kids I'd known since kindergarten to see. I had teachers who cared and a routine to follow, and now it was all coming to an end. Other kids had planned ahead for this, but I was too busy just getting through each day to be bothered figuring out a life plan.

When I graduated from high school, Linda told me I had to move out. "What are your plans?" she said one day. "You know you can't stay here."

She said it was because I was drinking too much, which might have been true. I had hit the point where I didn't want to work anymore, and I just wanted to drink and party all the time.

Don't ask me why I could see that drinking was so bad when my mom did it or my uncles did it, but I didn't see it the same when I did it. I don't know. I just saw it as completely separate things. It was a pity party for me some-times—"My life is so lousy that I deserve to drink," and sometimes I just couldn't see any other way to live.

My boyfriend moved away to Florida. I think we had broken up a million times by then anyway, and once again, I didn't have anywhere to go. And no car, either.

Everybody loves puppies, but nobody loves a dog. Well, now I was the dog, and nobody would return my calls. My relatives, who seemed to be around when I was little, were nowhere to be found. They all knew I was drinking and drugging and they weren't very eager to get involved with me.

A friend from my hometown, Brandy, invited me to come live with her in her college town—and that was pretty good, because she had parents and credit cards and I didn't. And since her parents were divorced and her dad lived out of state, well, she had double everything. I wore her clothes because I couldn't afford my own. She was supposed to be going to college, so I figured I might as well sign up, too, but the problem was that neither one of us could stop partying long enough to actually make it to class.

Cocaine became my great love affair. I could lose all track of time and feel invincible! It made me feel like Superwoman. And if I worked hard at it, I could probably shorten my time on this miserable planet while I was at it. I didn't do anything in moderation, so when I got high, I got high . . . for days and weeks at a time. I'd be in someone's swimming pool at seven in the morning and start to come down and realize I had no idea where I was.

We lived in an apartment, and neither one of us was working. We weren't doing anything, really, just partying. I could stay awake for days at a time, doing cocaine as easily as eating a bag of potato chips. One day would run into the next, and I'd lose all concept of time until the sun would rise again. Every day, we would take ecstasy and go to the beach. I was always the scapegoat when Brandy had to tell her parents why we were short on rent or in trouble.

The drugs gave me a temporary escape from my reality, but it all had aftereffects. When you're coming off a drug like ecstasy or coke, every bad thing you've ever done, every lie you've ever told, every person you've ever hurt, it all flashes before your eyes in two seconds. You're the plankton of the sea. So it's tempting to just stay high and avoid the guilt—which I did.

I would lie about how much coke I had done, trying to make it sound like I had done just a little. Other people would talk about how they needed to come down because they had to go somewhere or someone would be worried about them, so I made up those stories, too. I didn't actually have anywhere to go, and no one was pacing at home worrying about where I was, but I wanted to make believe I had a better life than I did, so I pretended. Most of my lies were centered around making people think I was okay, that I was happy, that I had a reason to come down.

They weren't elaborate stories. But if someone asked me, "Are you okay? Do you need to stay here tonight?" I'd just smile and say, "No, I'm fine. I have somewhere to go . . ." then go somewhere else to do more coke and repeat the cycle. Truly, I was miserable, but it was important to me to keep up this façade that I had more of a life than I did. I don't know why.

I thought about my grandma a lot, even when I tried not to. Over and over, I'd replay the same conversations and thoughts, hating myself for moving out and not being there with her at the end. Knowing that my relatives blamed me for leaving.

The guilt alone was a good enough reason to get high. Thinking straight all the time was exhausting. The more I thought about my grandmother and my relatives and my worthless life, the worse my migraines got. The sickness I felt inside came out as literal sickness. But all the pain didn't feel so real when I got high.

Then I finally hit my rock bottom.

For two weeks straight, I had been high on coke, just feeling sorry for myself and suicidal. I'm not sure if I slept at all. I was in the middle of a real crisis of faith about my life, thinking, *What am I living for? Bars and drugs?* Sure, some of it was fun, but it wasn't a life. It wasn't a reason to keep waking up. It was just a way of forgetting the misery for a while. I was turning out just like my uncles said I would, no better than the rest of them. So I decided to go for it: to test my limits and see how high I could get, for how long. My last hurrah.

And after two weeks of poisoning my body, I started to have a heart attack.

No, seriously. That's what it was. No doctor needed to tell me; I clutched my racing heart and knew that this was it. I was going to die. And you know what? All of a sudden, I didn't want to die after all. "Please, Lord, if you'll just let me live, I will never, ever do this again . . ." Same prayer every drunk says over the toilet after a hard night of drinking, only more desperate, because this was my *life* in the balance.

He kept up his end of the bargain, and I kept up mine. Immediately, my heart slowed down, and I had no desire ever to do it again. No withdrawal, no sickness, no cravings, no nothing.

But I didn't quit drinking. That wasn't part of the bargain, and I wasn't ready for that. How was I going to deal with my life without drinking? I mean, let's not get crazy now. And I decided my bargain didn't extend to other drugs, either. It was cocaine that I recognized I had a problem with; I didn't think it was a big deal to experiment with other things.

I could never afford my portion of the rent, so we got kicked out of apartments and just kept moving around. Somehow we ended up in Atlanta. It's really a blur, but I think it went something like this:

Brandy: Want to go to Atlanta?

Me: Okay.

There was no rhyme or reason to any of it. There was nothing waiting for us in Atlanta, but what did I have here? So I moved. As we drove out of town, I looked into the rear view mirror and knew I was never coming back.

Brandy got a job as a waitress in a bar, and every night, we'd go there and hang out and try to get someone to give us drugs. Then, if we needed money, we could always sell some of the drugs people gave us.

Without a car, it was hard for me to find a job. For a while, I worked at a medical clinic. It was sort of a "minor emergency" hospital, and I worked part-time, whenever they needed me. I liked the sense of responsibility, feeling like I had a place to go and something to do, but the pay was low and rent was expensive in Atlanta. I couldn't cover my bills with my paychecks—and besides, this work stuff was really cutting into my drinking time. So I quit.

By this time, I was drinking gin or vodka straight, no mixers. I could drink anything. I had no idea then what a hold drinking had over me. It was socially acceptable, and I didn't feel the guilt I used to feel after I came down off cocaine. Except one time.

Soon after we moved to Atlanta, my brother Bobby and his family came to town for something, and we made plans to get together at my house. I was at the bar with friends that night, and I knew my brother's family was supposed to show up at a certain time. I watched that time come and go, but I didn't leave the bar. I just stayed and got more and more drunk.

At some point, I thought, *Oh, I should leave now. They're waiting for me*, but then someone bought me a drink and it was more fun for me to stay in my pretend world than to kill my buzz and face my brother. So I never went home that night. I don't know where I stayed, but Bobby and his family stayed over in my apartment with my roommate waiting for me, and I didn't come back until the next morning.

No matter how much I loved my brother and his family, I chose my priorities that night. I chose to stay at that bar and drink rather than come home and see them, even though I hadn't seen them in a long time and didn't know when they'd ever be back. Once I started drinking, I didn't care about anything, and I would not stop at one or two drinks. I made some stupid excuse about where I was, but Bobby was clearly disappointed in me when I got back that morning. It was a real low point.

I knew then that I was a drunk. It made me feel like scum, but that didn't mean I stopped. Feeling like scum just made me want to drink more. It made me think of my uncles and how they would choose to drink over anything else, and how I was doing the same thing. I was in a drunken stupor for the next three or four years. My memory of those years is corroded; people and places and times are all mashed together in this alcoholic haze.

I got on-again off-again jobs in sports bars and night clubs. I'd wind up quitting or getting fired because I was too drunk or showing up late. Every few months, I'd get new roommates. Brandy ended up going back home at some point, but I stayed. I just hung around in bars and made friends and waited to see if someone would invite me to live with them. It was, "Hey, you're pretty cool. Do you want to get an apartment?"

If you watch a toddler who can't seem to get comfortable, you'll see him lie down in one spot, then another, getting irritable. He can't find the right person to hold him, or he's not wrapped tightly enough, and he just can't get situated, so he cries. That was me—I couldn't get situated. I felt like I was walking in circles trying to figure out where I could get comfortable. I had no safe haven, no home base to land. The ground kept shifting under me.

I lived with so many people during that time that I can't even remember all their names. My whole life was just a big toxic party. I skipped right past pot because it always just depressed me. I wasn't interested in the drugs that made me feel "mellow." I wanted to feel on the edge, super-awake, bold. It's a good thing I was afraid of needles, because I'm sure that shooting up would have been the ultimate. The danger of it didn't scare me; I just couldn't handle the thought of a needle going into my skin. So I stuck to what I knew best—drinking. I also tried a few new things like acid, crank, and extacy. I was always testing death.

At a bar one night, the owner of a strip club came over to me and told me I should come dance for him. My first thought was, *I was the homecoming queen . . . I can't be a stripper!* But then I had other thoughts. After all, I had worked a sports bar in short shorts and tiny tank tops . . . was it very different? It's not like I'd run into anyone I knew there—this was Atlanta, far from my little home-town. Maybe I could make some real money and get my own apartment. Maybe I wouldn't even get evicted this time. I mean, I could go to work drunk and no one would even mind. Heck, I could get drunk *at* work—perfect! So I accepted.

It was a very popular club in Atlanta where there were lots of dancers . . . and I was the only white one. I walked in with a big ole' smile, thinking, *These women are going to love me. This is going to be great!* That was naïve, to put it mildly. The fact that I was the only white girl there wasn't strange to me. I never saw color anyway. My friends were my friends and people were people.

My first day, I worked the day shift. It's still dark in the club during the day, but the atmosphere is a lot different than it is at night. You feel more on display.

I was embarrassed and nervous, and . . . embarrassed and nervous. I sat back to watch the other girls and quickly realized I didn't know how to move like they did. The owner would ask, "Are you ready to dance?" and I'd say, "No, let's wait until the next song." Maybe I could stall until the shift was over.

Eventually it came time, and I felt so awkward. Was I doing it right? What was I supposed to do with my body?

The women were less than pleased to see little Miss Disney princess in their club, and did their best to run me off.

"Why aren't you in a different club? Why do you need to work here?"

I didn't really have an answer, and they didn't deserve one anyway, so I'd just say something like, "Don't worry about that." They hated all the new girls, especially me.

They were expecting me to be a sweet little pageant girl, and they thought that if they just called me names and ridiculed me and cussed at me, I'd run out of there in tears. What they didn't know is that I had grown up fighting, and I decided they were not going to intimidate me. Deep down, I was hurt by the comments, but I would never let that show.

So we fought constantly, and I would not back down. I cussed at them and said ugly things right back. *I'll be damned if you're going to scare me out of here.*

I was determined to stay, and to earn my spot. In this club, it wasn't just about looking sexy—you had better know how to dance. And me? I didn't.

I didn't have any rhythm, and I wasn't really sure if I could learn. I sort of bought into the "white girls can't dance" idea. But I wasn't going to give in without a fight, so I would go to the club when no one was there but the DJ, and I'd practice my dancing.

"Listen to the music," he'd say. "Feel the beat. It doesn't matter how cute you are if you can't dance."

It was like Steve Martin in *The Jerk*. Out of nowhere one day, I got rhythm.

And little by little, I earned the women's respect. Like getting "jumped in" to a gang, once I made it clear that I wasn't leaving, they became my closest friends. I even moved in with some of them. Well, I slept on the floor with a pillow and blanket, but it was a place to take a shower and sleep, anyway.

Once the girls got to know me, and we quit fighting, it was a friendly atmosphere at the club. We'd sit at the tables and talk to the guys even when we weren't working, just because we ended up becoming friends with a lot of the customers.

After I gained confidence, I loved the attention, and I loved to dance. I'd buy cute clothes and get dressed up like I was going out with my friends to meet guys—which I pretty much was. While I was fixing my makeup in the mirror I had that same nervous excitement that you get when you know you look good and you're about to go out on the town.

There's a VIP room in the club, and the guys would send us in there to dance while they'd walk in and out and go off to buy drinks. Then they'd ask me to tell them at the end of the night how many times we danced so they'd know how much to tip us. I wasn't exactly Honest Abe, but they knew my friends would lie through their teeth, so they mostly asked me for the numbers.

"Tell them we danced two hundred times!" the girls would say.

"The DJ doesn't even have two hundred songs!"

I could have named myself anything I wanted—I could have become Candy or Trixie or any silly stripper name—but I had enough trouble without trying to remember what my name was supposed to be. So I was just Tracy.

Nobody there knew my story. I dated men, sometimes for long periods of time, and they never even knew my parents were dead. I'd just tell people that my family lived in a small

town a few hours south and leave it at that. Pity tips weren't
my style; I had gone through so much to escape my past that
I sure wasn't about to relive it every day so people would feel
sorry for me. That would have messed up the whole feeling
for me. I mean, I was getting paid to go to a bar and drink and
hang out with my friends and meet guys. Far as I could see,
that was a pretty sweet deal. Why wreck it with my sad story?

Mostly, I had a stereotypical male point of view about
relationships; I didn't want closeness and commitment, I
was just trying to fill up some emptiness inside. Sometimes,
I'd stay with someone and think the next day, *Why did I do
that?* I was way too carefree, and I am very lucky that I never
suffered repercussions from that. I think about that a lot.

It occurred to me that I had no connections anymore.
Every now and then, I called my brother, but most times I
would just get a lecture. I always hated to hear the sadness and
disappointment in his voice. One night, walking down the
street, I had a thought: *If I were to die right here, nobody would
even know.* I would have been a Jane Doe, toe-tagged as just
another drifter drug addict with no family. Who would identify my body? The men I was having one-night stands with?
No one would even know to notify Bobby. Who would care
if I overdosed right here in the middle of the street?

It was the most awful, lonely feeling. Everything was
meaningless. *I* was meaningless. If I had a funeral, there
would be a dozen strippers and a few customers in atten-
dance, and people would say, "Oh, how sad," and they'd all

go back to the club and get drunk that night, and the world would keep right on turning as if I never existed at all.

Holidays were depressing. My friends at the club all had families they could go to on Thanksgiving, Easter, Christmas. Going home to my relatives, I always just felt like an outcast and an inconvenience, so I quit going. I just tried to make the best of my situation in Atlanta.

In the beginning, the club gave me a schedule, but it was really flexible. There were so many girls working there that they never had to worry about someone missing a shift. If I wanted to take off for a week, I could. If I decided I didn't feel like dancing that night but I just wanted to drink and hang out, I could do that, too. It's not like there's a boss breathing down your neck and yelling at you for being late or taking breaks. You can disappear whenever you want, and you were always welcomed back.

When you're a stripper, you become your own traveling show. You can pretty much go anywhere and find work, so I did. Some of the girls from the club and I went on the road. We'd work a few weeks here, few weeks there, and move on again. We could always find work, because once you've been a stripper at the club we came from, that's like being a chef who trained at Le Cordon Bleu. No one's going to turn you down.

Sometimes we stayed on the streets. When I think back on it, though it felt like an adventure then, it's a wonder that I didn't get raped or killed. Kind of the way my mom believed it would be okay to leave me in bars when I was a little kid, I believed no one was going to bother me out on the streets. It might seem like naiveté, but it was really a deeper—almost irrational—trust. (I know it was God's care that kept me safe. It makes me laugh with joy to know this now.) We weren't afraid because we were hanging around with the people who everyone else was afraid of. It was during this period that I smoked crack for the first and last time. We got tired of being homeless, though, so we picked up and left again, traveling all over the country, from East St. Louis to Fort Lauderdale with just enough gas money to get us from town to town.

No matter where I moved or what I was up to, though, I was always trying to find a church to go to. My girlfriends thought I was crazy—"You're going out drinking and stripping all night and you want to be in church in the morning?" Well, yeah. "You're so weird."

And I knew they were right. Pretty much. It *was* weird, and I knew I was making bad choices, but I still had the same heart of that seven-year-old girl. Looking back, I think I was like Adam, hiding in the Garden of Eden. I wanted to hide from God, but I still wanted Him to be there when I called for Him. And He was.

You'd probably expect me to tell you now how awful I feel about these years and how much I hate what I did, but you know what? I didn't hate it. I loved it. Sin is fun. It wouldn't be tempting otherwise. We brought our little stripper road show to Miami, where I met a girl named Nikki, and she was only eighteen years old. The club was just horrible, girls prostituting themselves and getting treated with such disrespect, and suddenly I felt motherly. It killed me to see this sweet girl there, around things I knew she wasn't a part of, "If you're going to strip, come back to Atlanta with me. You don't have to be in a club like this." At least there, I knew she'd be safe.

We were thick as thieves after that, and we shared an apartment in Atlanta. I made pretty good money there, though I was terrible at managing it. Some of the women did a great job of saving up their money, but for the most part, that's a stripper's life—you make lots of money, but somehow you're always broke.

One day, I was watching a daytime talk show and I had one of those "aha" moments. There was a woman on the show talking sexual things that happened to her in her childhood, and it was a story something like mine. At that point I understood that anytime you touch a child in an affectionate way and think anything other than "that's a child," that's molestation.

Oh.

So it wasn't my fault.

You're probably thinking it's weird that it took me so long to get that, but that whole time, I never classified what happened to me as abuse or molestation. I didn't know what it was, really, but there had always been this nagging

feeling that I had brought it on myself, that I had something to feel guilty about. But here was the psychologist
telling the woman that it was not her fault. The host of the
show was agreeing with her, and they were both telling her
that it is never the child's fault.

I began to understand that anyone, especially a child, in
this type of situation is burdened with an immense amount
of guilt and shame. I felt ashamed of so much that went
on in my house, and during my childhood I felt like the
adults around me overlooked or ignored so many things.
Not only were bad things happening, but nobody defended
me. Plus, I never felt I had the right to speak up or an addi-
tional shame would be placed on me, the shame of "com-
plaining." I could imagine them saying, "Isn't there enough
drama already without you telling crazy stories and taking
everything so serious!" To be a child, defenseless, and feel
that you can't stand up for yourself because you would
stand alone, its horrible.

Growing up, no matter how intense or intrusive something was, if it could be pushed aside and forgotten, it was.
When I became a grown up and faced some of my own
demons, I found that many others were still living in a forced
forgetfulness. When I brought up the topic again with family I was accused of wanting to tarnish the family history and
reputation. In truth, I wasn't trying to place blame on anyone—I had formed my opinions about my uncles and no one
was going to talk me out of those. I just wanted someone to

say they believed me and admit how completely dysfunctional and wrong the household of my childhood was. I
needed to know it wasn't unreasonable for wanting closure.
But in response I got, "Was it really that bad?"

How bad is bad enough?

Well, the TV earned its worth that day when it convinced me that it wasn't my fault. That it was bad enough
and I needed to do something about it.

This anxiety built up inside me until I thought I was
going to boil over. I had to go see my uncle. After all these
years, I had to confront him. So I told Nikki that we had to
go right then and there, and we got in her car and drove for
miles and miles.

I pulled up at their old, shingled house and Len was sitting
on the back steps, drunk and staring at the car. As I walked
toward him he looked like he was seeing a ghost. This man
who had been so huge and intimidating to me my whole life
now looked like a weak, little, old man. I walked up and sat
on the step beside him. I was not afraid. I knew there was
nothing he could do to me. There were a million things I
wanted to say, questions I wanted to ask. Why was he so mean
to me? Why did he hate me and my brothers? What had I
ever done to him to make him want to hurt me?

I wanted to tell him how angry I was, how, as a little girl,
I prayed that he would die. I wanted to be the grown up
now and make him feel inferior. I wanted to yell at him the
way he always yelled at me! But right then, none of it would

come out. Instead, I looked at him and calmly said, "I want you to know that I forgive you for what you did to me." I paused and continued, "But I would be lying if I didn't say that I hoped you would burn in hell." He sat there just staring at me, tears streaming down his face with an almost pathetic look on his face. Part of his expression said "I'm sorry," and the other part, which I had seen a million times, "You little bitch! Don't you talk to me like that!" The look did not scare me anymore.

No more words were exchanged. I got up and walked back to the car. I never even looked back at him. I left there feeling that I had taken a huge step. I would never forget all the times that he scared me and made my life hell, but it felt good to face him and know that he could not scare me anymore.

We went to a football game at my old high school that night, and drove back to Atlanta the next day.

Nikki and I were best friends and went out every night. She was as close to family as I had. Even though she had her own family, sometimes she stayed with me on holidays, and we'd try to have little holiday dinners at our place. She was good for me; she didn't do drugs. However, she did drink, so we did that very well together. I worked days at the apartment building where we lived, answering phones and doing secretarial work, and nights at the club.

Then, in the spring of 1993, we went to Dallas to visit a guy I was dating, and I thought, *This is a nice place*. I visited a strip club there, and couldn't believe what I was seeing—

all these women just standing there flipping their hair around and making a fortune! They had it so easy. At the clubs I worked at, you really had to dance for your money.

They're not even moving, I thought. *These girls don't have to do anything!*

Sweet.

"I'm moving to Dallas," I told Nikki.

"I'll move with you," she said. "I don't have anything here."

Everything we owned fit into her car, so we just took off. We didn't have an apartment when we got there, so we just stayed in a hotel for a while. I know it was April of 1993 because we were in that hotel when the Branch Davidian suicides at Waco were all over the news, and I thought, *Uh-oh. Are Texans crazy people?*

We found work at a club that was nice and safe. Sometimes, you're safer working at a really nice strip club than you are at a regular bar. Waitresses don't have bouncers watching over them. Strip clubs aren't always what people imagine them to be. I'm not condoning it or saying it's a dream job, but a lot of the time, being a stripper is like being a therapist—just without clothes. Guys come in and just want someone to talk to. It sounds lame, but it's true. There were always girls who did things that allowed men to degrade them, but for me, I decided it was my job. I did my work and went home. I wasn't going to belittle myself for anyone. I know that sounds funny, considering that I was taking my clothes off for a living, but I thought, *I'm getting*

paid to dance for three and a half minutes, and you're paying to
watch me. Who's the fool?

I was always quick to lay out the rules before I would
dance for someone. I was very girly and didn't do the whole
black-leather thing. The old-time burlesque shows were
my inspiration; there's something to be said for leaving
something to the imagination. I wouldn't hesitate to tell
someone no if they were asking for something that made
me uncomfortable. It didn't matter to me if I was dancing
for guys who were young and cute or hideous to look at,
but it did matter if they were rude. And if I felt like someone was crossing the line, I sure would say something—and
not in such polite words, either.

"Is it possible for a stripper to be a complete prude?" my
friend asked me. "Because you are."

After the way I grew up, never having a chance to take a
stand, this felt like my time to claim my boundaries. Even
though I was compromising my morals just being there, there
were things I would not compromise. I felt okay about my job
as a stripper, but if I let customers tell me what to do with my
body, what did that make me? Between the customer and me,
I was the smart one—which is the truth in any strip club, I
think. No one was going to make me feel dirty or powerless.
Not the customers or my bosses or the other women.

The women in the club certainly weren't about to intimidate me. "Honey, you don't know where I've been and
what I've seen. You can't scare me."

Mostly, though, the men were very polite to me, not crossing any lines. I was always talking, whether I was dancing or sitting at a table. Lots of guys would come in just to talk, not even wanting me to dance. We'd talk about sports, music, life, whatever.

Sometimes, the same men who were perfectly polite to me were the ones who caused trouble with the other girls. I think the difference was these conversations. The more I talked, the more I became a real person to them, not just a stripper.

Men from all different backgrounds would come into the club, from politicians to preachers. I was always curious what a preacher was doing in a strip club—was he trying to save somebody's soul? Backstage, I was always talking to the girls about faith in God, and they would cry and tell me about their miserable lives. It's probably surprising to hear that faith is even discussed in that atmosphere, but it was discussed a lot. It made me sad to think that there were so many people who didn't know that God loved them the way that I knew He did. My heart hurt for other people who didn't understand the grace that God has.

Listening to them made me appreciate the relationship I had with God. We were all sort of lost and pitiful, but I had this source of comfort that they didn't have. Maybe no one had ever told them before. Maybe I was a drunk stripper, but I was a good-hearted drunk stripper.

When you're dancing for a living and doing shots so you forget you're sleeping on someone's couch, you can feel like God has forgotten you or that you're unredeemable. You feel judged, and you try to get tough to it. You pretend you don't care what anyone says or thinks—but the truth is you do. It felt good to tell these women that the Lord would never, ever forget them or stop loving them, and that His grace is forever.

The reminder wasn't bad for me, either. Some days I just felt like I was in quicksand, sinking into this hopeless never-ending hole. I wasn't proud of where I was, and I didn't see a future. Part of me believed that God meant great things for me, but I had no idea how I would ever get there. Sometimes, I just wanted to close my eyes and not be on this Earth anymore; it was such a painful place.

But the funny thing is that this was the most stability I'd had in my life since my grandmother died. I finally had a job I actually liked, I had some money, and I had quit doing most everything except drinking. According to my expectations, that was pretty good. I had very nearly forgotten that the Lord might have wanted something more from me.

— *Six* —

IT WAS TOWARD THE END OF MY STRIPPING YEARS that Jesus spoke to me onstage. There I was, leaning over to take a tip from a handsome man, when I heard Him say, "This is the man you're going to marry."

Excuse me? "Jesus! Don't talk to me when I'm on stage!"

But He was adamant. "That's your husband."

"I am not looking for a husband, Jesus. Now leave me alone. I'm busy here."

I finished my act and the guy ended up at a table with Nikki, who was trashed.

"Tracy, come do a shot with us!" she called out. Like I would refuse? So I sat down with them and got to talking, and the guy was very nice, but I wasn't looking to meet my future husband that night. I knew Jesus had to be wrong— or maybe I had heard him wrong—because the man was already married.

"So what are you doing here if you're married?" I grilled

him, because that's what I did. Why should the guys ask all the questions? I always wanted to know why people were there.

But it turned out his wife worked out of town and had an agenda that didn't include him, and his buddies had taken him out to get his mind off her. Bryan was his name, and he was a Texas gentleman, and I soon figured out that we had a lot in common. We ended up becoming friends.

Or, to be more accurate, best friends . . . after a while, at least. I told Bryan everything in my life. I told him about everyone I'd ever dated, places I'd been, mistakes I'd made, and all the crazy things my girlfriends and I did. I was dating an idiot at the time, and I'd talk to Bryan about him, too. We'd call each other and laugh and talk for hours sometimes.

He owned his own company, which he had started about four years before we met. At one point, he used to work for a guy in the advertising business and Bryan had an idea to start a company with ad specialty items geared toward high school athletics programs, which the boss thought was a very stupid idea. After Bryan got fired, he borrowed seven thousand dollars and started his company—which became very successful. That was no lucky break, though; Bryan's the sort of guy who started doing odd jobs and mowing lawns when he was about eleven. He grew up hard, like me, and his ambition was strong. There was no way he would ever let himself fail at anything.

He always told me that I was a good person, and that life had more to offer me, definitely more than working in a strip club. I really started to buy into what he said to me, and I began to see life differently. He gave me advice about the guy I was dating and never could understand why I was with him—the guy treated me very badly. I asked him the same question about his wife.

He was so respectful and never wanted anything from me, but we were getting so close it scared me, so I did my usual act of running away.

I went back to my hometown for two weeks, not really knowing whether I was going to stay there or go back to Dallas, not really knowing what my purpose was in being there. I hopped from house to house crashing on people's couches, and I took a long look at the path I was on and what my future would hold if I stayed in my hometown. Bad memories, no opportunities. There had to be more to life. So I started thinking then that it might be time to make some changes. I was twenty four years old, and still didn't have any roots. Every couple of months I moved around again, staying with this person and that. Drinking was the only real constant in my life.

What was I doing here? It was as if I was resisting any kind of stability. Back in Dallas, I had a few great friends and a job where I made good money and the managers treated me like family. It might not have been the perfect path, but it was a start, and it was time I learned how to build a life. I called the manager of the club where I worked and he bought my plane ticket back to Texas. I never looked back.

A woman I met co-signed on a loan for my apartment, and I paid the whole lease upfront so I wouldn't have to worry about messing up paying my rent.

The apartment was small—just one bedroom—so it didn't need a lot of furniture. For the first time, I felt like I was on the right track. I felt like I was somebody. I tried to be financially responsible this time. For that, I needed a system, so I would take envelopes and write labels on them: "Grocery," "Electric," "Water," and so on. At the end of the work night, I would put some money in each envelope.

I loved coming home to my apartment. It was a gated community where I felt very safe. I hung wallpaper in the bathroom, bought a bed-in-a-bag set from Target, and put out a "Welcome" mat by the front door. Nikki rented an apartment in the same complex so we could be right near each other again.

Life was good, except that I was still drinking too much, and that bothered me. I managed to be more responsible, but I was still a functioning drunk. Standing in front of the mirror, I realized how tired I looked. It was the blood that finally did it, though. February 2—and you know that's an important date, because I don't remember dates—after drinking at work, I threw up blood, and felt the generational curse playing me like a violin. Enough.

I asked the bartender to serve me tonic and let me pretend to have a buzz at the club. "What?" he asked. "I'm not drinking," I said. He didn't faint dead away, but I'm guessing he was waiting for the punch line.

Quitting drinking was the hardest thing I've ever done. I had never worked sober, and nothing seemed funny anymore. The jokes, the comments, the dancing . . . it seemed pathetic, not fun. How was I going to get through this?

I remember thinking, *It's been one day since I drank. It's been a week.* Then a month, then three months. Then I quit counting. I didn't go to group meetings or therapy or anything; fear was my motivator. When I saw that blood, I thought, *I can't be like her. This isn't how I'm meant to go.*

I got back in touch with Bryan and was glad to tell him how responsible I was becoming. He was proud, but said he'd be more proud if I had another job. From the first day we met he had told me I didn't fit in where I was working.

He was right, of course. I tried to figure out what I would do from here; I told myself that twenty-five was my cut-off year. I wasn't going to be one of those ninety-year-old strippers who keeps up her act until she has to walk out on stage with a cane.

To relieve some of the stress of quitting drinking, I began exercising. I became a workout fanatic, trying to get down to a minute size. I lost so much weight that everyone was starting to tell me I looked sick, though.

Bryan would ask if I'd gone to the grocery store and tell me I needed to eat. He'd show up to take me out to eat lunch because he was convinced I wasn't eating. Normally, we went out with friends—his friends, my friends, whoever was around. We went to fun places where I would try new things. I had never heard of bisque before, but I wound up loving it. Another time, he asked if I wanted soufflé, and I said, "I hate fancy stuff. I don't eat fancy foods." When this gorgeous chocolate soufflé came, I took a bite and loved it, and he said, "No, no, you don't like fancy food. Don't eat the soufflé."

I wasn't sure about table etiquette, and he was so sure of himself that it made me nervous. I would ask him which fork I was supposed to use, and he'd say it didn't matter. He was the kindest man I'd ever been around. *Could it be possible for a man to be this nice to me for no reason?* I wondered.

But why question it? I could see he was sad when he talked about his marriage. I always joked about my relationships and laughed it off, but the truth was I was tired of being with someone just for lack of something better. I wanted someone to love me and be good to me and really be around in my life, not just someone to talk to on the phone and visit in other cities.

One day Bryan showed up at my house and said, "I have to tell you, I asked her for a divorce." After ten years of trying to make things work in his marriage, he had finally given up.

Well, that changed everything. Here was my best friend, my "safe" friend, in my apartment, telling me he was single. It felt very strange, and I didn't know what to make of it.

Bryan had a hard time with the idea of divorce, not because he was pining away for this woman, but because it really shattered his idea of what his life was supposed to look like at that point. He was a successful businessman, but the marriage that was supposed to be forever had fallen apart—he had no kids, and he felt like a failure. He was depressed and drinking too much and trying to figure out what to do with his life from there.

My friends said, "You should go out with him," but I was afraid to mess things up. However, I had broken up with the idiot I was dating.

Bryan showed up with a package. The card said, "I thought we would do something totally weird, like go on a real date, and I didn't want you to say you didn't have anything to wear."

In the package: a dress, shoes, and a purse. I didn't know what to do. Going out with someone who knows everything about you, who you can truly be yourself with . . . there's a concept. We went to a jazz bar, then he took me to see some sculptures in a fountain—this famous landmark in Dallas. This wasn't something I did all the time. In fact, I'd never done it before. Bryan was into culture. He knew so much about art and music and everything that it intimidated me. I was just stubborn and asked, "Why are we here? Why did you bring me to see a fountain with some horses in it?"

He said, "So you can enjoy it. I thought we could sit here and talk."

We had a nice time, but I was nervous. He walked me to my door and wished me good night.

A few dates later, he slipped an antique diamond ring on my finger, shaped like a tiara. "If you're going to be a princess, you need to let me treat you like one," he said.

And that's just what he did. I have never met anyone who is more gentlemanly than Bryan. All the little things, he does. Even if we were just hanging out with his friends, Bryan would always open doors for me and pull out my chair for me—he knew all the polite things to do. And he said Texas stuff like "Darlin'," which I loved. He had such an inner confidence about him that I admired.

And still, I pulled away from him. Maybe he was too nice. All the things that had been told to me in my childhood crept up. Maybe he was too good for me. Why would he want to date me? This seemed too good to be true. So I let him know that I wanted to be friends, but didn't want to commit to a relationship. I was scared of him being too close and of getting hurt, but in trying to protect myself, I was purposely pushing away the nicest man I'd ever known.

So he took off and went to the Bahamas. He was there for a few weeks when I realized I was probably making a mistake. What if he met someone in the Bahamas? How would I feel if he was going out with someone else? Maybe I really was supposed to be with him. After all, God did say I would marry him. Would I really hate being treated like a princess?

I called him on Thanksgiving and asked him to come back to Texas. He said he was not coming back if I was still going to be indecisive. He said if I didn't want to be with him, that was fine, but if I did, I had to stop pushing him away because it was hurting his feelings. I agreed, and he came home. I knew I loved him, and he loved me, and we both knew this was our destiny.

Christmas was coming, so we did some shopping together. My favorite thing was this music box he bought to put under his grandma's tree. I had never seen the kind of beautiful decorations that people put out for Christmas, like train sets and nativity sets. This music box had a Christmas scene inside. It was so special, and I could listen to the music for hours.

I had a little tree in my apartment, cute and decorated. I wanted to have a real Christmas, and I finally felt like I wasn't imposing on other people's holiday with their families. This was my apartment and my tree and my new boyfriend to celebrate with. He bought me so many gifts that they were piled higher than the tree. His other Christmas present to me was that I didn't need to work all of December. The best gift, though, was the experience with him. Getting to spend a real Christmas with his family was something I'll never forget.

We moved in together in January. The lease on my apartment was up anyway. We both knew we were going to get married, so there was no big elaborate proposal down on one knee . . . one night in bed, he just handed me a box with a wedding ring in it.

To this day, he says that if I hadn't "come to my senses" and agreed to be with him, he would have sold his company and moved to an island somewhere and made a living selling coconut drinks. I believe him, too, because he was at the same low point I was when I was walking down the street imagining my empty funeral: He didn't have any real connections. This gave him a second chance to build his ideal life.

Bryan wasn't very much into church, but he knew it was important to me to find a good church to join before we got married.

He had a friend who played piano at a great piano bar in Dallas, and the man would always invite Bryan to visit his church, which was a nondenominational charismatic church. We decided to check it out on Easter Sunday. Bryan was raised Methodist, and I was raised southern Baptist. But Bobby was Pentecostal, and I was accustomed to seeing people worshipping with their hands in the air. Bryan wasn't. He didn't know what to think. It felt good to know something he didn't know. I laughed—after all those times I was mad at Bobby for making me go to church, it paid off. At that moment, I was so glad I'd been exposed to it so I could explain something to Bryan. Our whole relationship, he'd been the one who knew everything.

"They all just want your money," he had said on the way to church.

As soon as the preacher began talking about tithing and how God would bless you if you tithed, Bryan started elbowing me.

He told me to give the church all the money in our

checking account. It was like a challenge to God from Bryan, to see if this preacher was telling the truth. I wrote a check for every dime in the account. The next week, we had our biggest accounts receivable week ever, which more than made up for the money we'd given away.

Every week, Bryan would test God, questioning the church and trying to figure out if this was for real.

"God doesn't need to prove himself to any man," I told him, "But He will meet you where you need to be met. He'll show you He's real."

We got married in April. We picked a chapel with stained glass that looked like a music box. My dress was gorgeous—very feminine and very southern. I was very nervous, and so was Bryan. Bobby walked me down the aisle to give me away, and Nikki was my Maid of Honor. A couple of my family members were there at our small wedding. The sun came through the stained glass windows and the whole chapel glowed. It was all very surreal with the colors from the stained glass, the roses, and the Lord's prayer sung a cappella. It was a perfect dream.

We had the reception in a hotel, where we hung ferns and had sweet tea, because that's Bobby's favorite. I bought the wedding cake at a grocery store because I thought it was silly to spend a lot of money on a cake, but maybe that wasn't the best idea. The top tier fell off as we cut it.

After that, we went on a cruise to Puerto Rico for our honeymoon. Eight days after saying "I do," I got pregnant.

When we got home to Dallas, I just knew I felt weird. I was so into exercise that I knew when my body was "off," and it was off. Bryan went to buy a pregnancy test, and I refused to believe the results—so he went back and got another, along with a candy bar.

"The way you're acting, you're either pregnant or you're PMSing," he said. "This should cover it either way."

By the end of the day, I had taken seven pregnancy tests. And then I realized . . . okay, I'm pregnant. *Oh my goodness, I'm pregnant!*

"What did I do?" I thought. It was all so fast, and such a huge change all at once, that I began doubting my decision. Marriage is always an adjustment—dealing with in-laws and figuring out how to communicate with each other and make compromises and think of another person's needs before your own. I was used to being the center of attention, making my own money, and suddenly I was supposed to be the happy suburban housewife. One month, I was shopping for lingerie to dance in, and the next, I was in the maternity section feeling lost and scared.

I have no idea how to be a mom, I thought. *What if I stink at it?*

Morning sickness was not kind to me, either. I spent most of those first few months in bed or in the bathroom, and I was a living, breathing mood swing. That wasn't easy on Bryan. When you're carrying around as much baggage as the two of us were, the marriage adjustment can really push you to your limits—but adding in an unexpected pregnancy so soon turned it into a surreal experience.

We had all these plans that had to be scrapped immediately. We had planned to go to Fiji for my birthday, to Vegas just for the heck of it . . . and now all travel plans were indefinitely on hold. Bryan had married this shapely, spontaneous girl who loved to travel and party, and everything changed in eight days.

I got large fast by sleeping and eating the days away. I loved feeling this baby inside of me, and sometimes I would just feel so happy—but this other part of me was such a killjoy! My insecurities mounted as the months went on. Bryan did all the shopping for my maternity clothes—he would go out and bring home bags of clothing for me— because I was self-conscious about my weight and feeling pretty lousy. Not a lot of husbands would do that, I think. It was cute to see what he would bring home.

On one of the checkups, the doctor said he was worried that the baby might have Down syndrome and did an amniocentesis. Then he said we wouldn't know the results for three weeks. Three weeks! I nearly miscarried because of all the stress of having this big question mark in the air. I could have handled it, but the strain of not knowing is always the worst part. The results came back normal . . . and we found out we were having a boy.

That's when the really crazy thoughts began.

What if I become an abuser?

People who are sexually abused become sexual abusers. That's what I always heard, and it's what I believed. I don't know any more why I internalized this so deeply. Maybe my uncle told me this when I was younger, and I carried it with me like a curse. Deep inside me was this twisted worry that I was going to sexually abuse a child, the way he had abused me. In my mind, it was like cancer or heart disease; if it runs in the family, you probably will get it, too. Just something terrible you inherit.

The first time I felt that worry so strongly was when my friend's son was born. I loved him, but I really struggled being around him, especially when she changed his diaper. I didn't want to look or to be close to him. My friend noticed the way I was uncomfortable. "How come you won't ever change him?" she asked me, and I tried to shrug it off with an excuse.

But one time I finally had to, and I filled up with worry. *What if it's true?* I thought. *What if I am going to be a sexual predator?*

The kid had a dirty diaper, though, and I was babysitting him. What was I supposed to do? I changed him. And immediately, I realized . . . *Oh, how stupid!* No, I didn't have any horrible urges or perverted feelings. I was changing this little boy, and no monster inside me was going to leap out and hurt him.

How would I feel when it was my own boy, though? I prayed that I would be a good mom and never hurt my son. I remembered how much my brothers loved our mother, even though she wasn't always there for them in the end, and I prayed I would do better than that.

Bryan bought me a four-door BMW that was a great "Mom car" and put a stroller in the back. We went to Babies "R" Us, Toys "R" Us, The Gap . . . it was fun getting ready and dreaming about this little person growing inside me.

Bryan had always made me feel so secure that he would always take care of me and this new baby. In those early days the business was still growing, and it was like anyone starting a business—there's a period of struggle and too many long nights, but we always had everything we needed and more.

He never believed in buying things on credit or spending more than we had, so sometimes he would say, "We can't get that yet," but there was never a doubt in my mind that someday we were going to have everything we wanted. He's so intelligent and hardworking, and everything he did became a success. For a while, Bryan wanted to believe that our success was all our own doing, but eventually he believed that God was granting him favor.

One of his policies is that he would never ask any of his workers to do something he wouldn't do himself, so I remember a time when I was very pregnant and the dryers in our warehouse were on the fritz. So on this hot summer day, we went to the warehouse and spent the whole afternoon with hairdryers in our hands drying the printing on the promotional products that needed to be shipped out.

Just three weeks before the baby was born, we moved

into the first house we built together. It was the nicest place I'd ever lived in.

And when the big day came, the baby didn't waste any time. We got to the hospital, and the doctor said it would be a while. Bryan was a nervous, pacing wreck, so the doctor told him to go get something to eat because this could be a long day. So Bryan left, but something made him decide to turn around. When he got back, things were moving faster than expected. The baby was ready, and I was in pain.

"You need to get in here!" Bryan literally grabbed the anesthesiologist from out of someone else's room, while he was tending to another patient. No *way* was I going through this without drugs.

Once the epidural kicked in, I felt a lot better, and the whole thing was over in less than two hours. It all went so fast that I don't even think the doctor had time to put scrubs on; he seriously just ran in the room in time to catch the baby.

"You were made to have babies," he told me. And just like everyone says, the minute they put that little boy in my arms, the pain was already just a memory.

We named him Jacob just because we liked the name. At the time, we had no idea how well the name would fit him, this perfect little angel in my arms.

I don't even know this little person, I thought. How could it be, then, that he felt like the most important thing in my life?

"I've only just met you," I said to Jacob, "But I love you more than anyone or anything in this world."

The weather was bad on the day we brought him home. It was pouring down rain, and I was in the back seat with Jacob. Bryan was so nervous driving in the rain, in the traffic, and it's funny how we never seemed to worry before. We had driven that same road a thousand times in the rain and in traffic and never thought about it twice, but now we had this precious cargo, and that changed everything.

We brought him home to his nursery, where we had a beautiful wooden cradle waiting for him. But after all the time we spent making him a nursery and filling it with furniture, he never actually slept in it. He slept in our room, either in his bassinet or in our bed with us. I loved having him close. It felt safe with the three of us in the same room. To me, it was like us against the world. When we went to sleep at night, I knew the two people I loved most in the world were safely tucked in next to me. When Jacob got his first "big bed," which was shaped like a car, we dragged that into our room, too.

I took a little heat from girlfriends who seemed horrified that I would have my son sleeping in the room with us, but it seemed unnatural to me *not* to have him there. I had slept in the same bed as my grandma until I was sixteen.

Bobby and his wife came and stayed with us after Jacob was born, to help out. They were so proud. I would lay in bed with Jacob and think how I was going to be responsible for this baby for the rest of his life. That was so scary and so exciting all at once.

Jacob was born already grown, it seemed. His birth was a great example of what was to come. It was as if he knew I was in pain, so he was trying to come out as quickly as possible. He is a pleaser, very efficient and well mannered, never wanting to cause anyone trouble. I didn't even need to child-proof the house—never needed to block the outlets or tell him not to stick coins in his mouth. He was smart and sweet and looked like Bryan.

How freeing it was to love him just to love him, and real-ize that there was no curse on me. I looked at my son and celebrated inside because I knew that what I went through would never happen to him. I knew his dad and I would never do anything to harm him. He was never going to see lamps being broken and tables getting smashed to pieces. He was never going to have to cower in fear while the people who were supposed to protect him gave each other black eyes and cussed at him and told him what a loser he was.

When Jacob was young, my aunt called to tell me that my uncle Len died. I said, "I'm sorry," and after hanging up, my first worry was, "What if no one sends flowers to his funeral?" Bryan was very confused as to why I'd even con-sider that. But after all that time, my first thought wasn't, *I hate him and I hope he's in* hell. I was able to feel sorry for him in that moment.

What a comfort to know that the madness had stopped with me.

— Seven —

WHEN JACOB WAS TWO, WE DECIDED HE NEEDED a sibling. I got pregnant again, and Jacob loved this baby in my belly so much. He would sing to the baby and lay his head on my belly and listen and wait for movements. We had another baby boy, Elijah. I thought I was lucky with our first angelic child, but here was another, just as sweet and well-behaved.

You always wonder how you could ever possibly love another child as much as you love your first. I worried about that, but when I looked at Elijah, I felt the same overwhelming love I had felt for Jacob. Elijah looked more like me, and you could tell instantly that he was going to have a strong personality and his own way of doing things. The fact that I was in labor for ten hours let me know that right off the bat.

Bryan brought Jacob to the hospital to see his new brother. He was so excited to hold him, to rub his head and kiss him. Finally, he could touch this baby he had been waiting to meet for so long.

I had dreamed of living in a Georgia-style mansion with big white columns and a winding staircase, and that's what Bryan built me. We moved in right after Elijah was born. It was my dream because I had always seen those houses decorated at Christmas, and I couldn't think of anything more beautiful. Our first Christmas there I put so many lights on the columns that we almost short-circuited the whole neighborhood.

By now, my relationship with my relatives had changed. We went to visit them on holidays, and a few times throughout the year we stayed with Bobby and his family. Taking my sons to the same grocery store I went to with my grandma brought back memories. No need for credit now. My grandma would have been so proud and loved my kids so much.

Maybe I was trying to prove to all my relatives that I was good, that I was not a failure after all. I had a great husband, great boys, money, a big house . . . wasn't I good enough now? I wanted them to approve of me, and I wanted to paint a prettier picture of what things had been like during my youth. Bryan often thought I was letting my relatives off the hook too easily, though. I'd tell him about the Easter baskets and the roller skates that my relatives would give me, and he'd say, "Was that enough to clear his conscience?"

The older I got, the more I realized Bobby always had my best interests at heart. I knew how hard and long he prayed for me. He loved me like I was his own child, and now he was so proud to see the life I was building.

Bryan considered him his own brother and admired him because of the way he lived what he believed. Bryan wanted to be extremely passionate about his faith the way Bobby was. He wanted to believe wholeheartedly.

Before Bryan really understood, he would say with wonder, "Your brother's in church all the time!" Then we went to Bobby's church with him, and Bryan got to see the way that Bobby worshipped, speaking in tongues with his arms in the air, very passionate about his worship. When we left, he said, "If I felt the way Bobby felt in church, I'd be there every time the doors were open too!" He says that if not for Bobby, he wouldn't be where he is in his faith.

Jacob started going to school in the mornings at age two-and-a-half. He loved school, and Elijah loved being with me. That Halloween, I took Jacob to the store to pick out a costume. He was Superman, and he dressed his brother up as McDonald's French fries. As they got older, they loved to play ball together, loved cartoons, loved playing make-believe games. Elijah followed Jacob around like a shadow.

Jacob always had interest in learning about different cultures, and he had taken a particular interest in African tribes. One day, they came down the stairs in their underwear triumphantly covered in markers. Jacob had colored himself and his baby brother with all different colored markers. Jacob proudly said, "Mom, we're tribal men." Elijah stuck his tongue out, and Jacob had even colored the child's tongue.

I put them in the tub to wash off the markers that night, and Jacob said to me in all seriousness, "I wonder if the tribal man's mom has to do this every night to him."

Jacob said he was going to marry me, and his dad said that wasn't possible because he was already married to me. Jacob learned to ride his bike in the cul-de-sac in front of the home, and it brought back so many memories. The Mother's Day cards, the hugs and kisses, the sweet nature they both have, watching Barney together again and again . . . every day was precious.

I do not deserve these kids, I thought. *They are better people than I will ever be.*

But I tried, obsessively, to become worthy of them. I wanted to be the perfect mother, to cook every meal for them, be there every time they fell, read to them, and be with them every minute of the day. I wanted their experiences growing up to be everything my own childhood wasn't. They needed to know that they came first in my life, and that I would always protect them and take care of their needs, and say and do all the right things. Every day I fell short of this Perfect Mom and Perfect Wife ideal I had set up in my head. And that caused all kinds of problems in our marriage, because I was mad at myself and taking things out on Bryan.

The devil never wanted Bryan and me to be married. He was going to ensure that we would drive each other crazy and try to separate us.

People sometimes ask me how I can believe in a loving

God when so many bad things happen in the world. Well, as much as I know Jesus exists, I also know the devil exists. If you put the two of them up against each other, Jesus would always win out, but that doesn't stop the devil from trying his best to get a stronghold on people. Some people believe the devil will show up on the front porch in a red suit like a Halloween costume, but he can look nice, sound nice, and make you think he's your friend.

I don't believe that God meant for me to be an orphan. I don't believe His plan was to have my parents both become alcoholics, or for my mom to throw away her life the way she did. I don't think He wanted me to live with abusive men or for my brother to wind up in prison. I think those are all choices that each of them made because they weren't listening to God's plans. Somewhere along the way, they turned away from Him and decided they knew better than He did what they should be doing.

People have free will, so they get to decide whether or not to listen to God every moment of the day. My parents had an amazing destiny given to them. I certainly don't think God decided, "Hey, wouldn't it be cool if this sweet, beautiful woman became a drunk and her three young kids would get to watch her become a pathetic person and die of liver disease?" But they chose to turn away from their calling and let the devil get a stronghold on them.

God is omnipresent, but the devil and his demons aren't. If the devil is intruding in your life or sending his demons out to bother you, there must be a good reason he wants to take you down, or he wouldn't spend his time on you. You must be doing something right, or he'd be off bugging someone in China or Australia instead.

Sometimes it's when you're starting to live out your destiny the way God wants it that the devil gets the most frantic. I picture him with legs spinning like in a Bugs Bunny cartoon, rushing here and there trying to destroy everything he can as quickly as he can.

On the outside, Bryan and I looked like Ken and Barbie—a perfect couple living a privileged life, going to church every Sunday with our perfect kids. We prayed all the time. We loved the Lord, but for about five years, we hated each other. And for the stupidest reasons. An argument that started, "I can't find the car keys," would end, ". . . we shouldn't even be together in the first place!"

Bryan's business—the one everyone said was a silly idea— turned out to be not such a silly idea after all. We produce all kinds of custom imprinted items, but our specialty is school-spirit products. Foam hands, clappers, seat cushions, blankets, umbrellas, megaphones, sports bottles . . . businesses buy the items so they can put their advertisements on them, and they provide them to schools at no cost.

It grew to be one of the largest ad specialty companies in the United States. I always expected it would be. I don't mean that to be smug, but I trusted that the Lord was going to bless us because we had honored Him by tithing and blessing other people. We had more fun doing things for others than we did for ourselves.

The main problem was that I had no idea what to do with myself when this trust was rewarded. I felt fake and wrong as a spoiled little housewife.

I still shopped at the same places I shopped when I was single and continued buying cheap clothes instead of brand-name stuff. I knew I didn't have to, but part of me felt like a sellout. It felt like I was *supposed* to struggle, and that if I had money I was forgetting where I came from. I thought that having nice things was going to automatically turn me into a snob.

Bryan had very different ideas about spending than I did. I had always bought "disposable" things. He, on the other hand, would save up his money when he was in high school and buy himself one pair of slacks and one blazer. They would be expensive—the nicest slacks and blazer he could find—and then he'd wear that all the time. He always had a taste for nice things, quality things, and he'd rather save up to do things right than buy lesser things. He was always thinking about the future, even as a kid.

His mom didn't have money, and they lived in an apartment in a bad area near Dallas when he was growing up. Early on, he decided he was never going to be poor when he grew up. He wanted a better life, and he was going to do whatever it took to accomplish that.

So when I'd go out and buy cheap shoes, then complain

about how my feet hurt, Bryan would ask, "Why do you keep buying these cheap shoes? You can afford better now. Spend the money and your feet won't hurt."

But I just didn't know what my role in life was supposed to look like. Now that I was a wife and a mother, did it mean I was supposed to shop at conservative stores and wear turtlenecks? Was I supposed to forget all my friends and just hang out with church ladies and my affluent neighbors?

Mostly, I felt like a kept woman, and wasn't so sure I wanted to be caged.

I'm not going to change. This is how I am, I thought. *I've struggled and fought my whole life, and I don't need a man to sweep me off my feet and control me.*

The thing is, Bryan wasn't even trying to control me. He just wanted to take care of me. But I had a fierce independent streak and kept feeling like I had something to prove to the world, like I had to keep struggling even though there was no more need to.

My anxiety just kept growing until I started having anxiety attacks, coupled with catastrophic thinking. I was absolutely convinced that something horrible was going to happen at any moment, every day. Some days, I thought my kids were going to die. And I'd worry about what would happen to the kids if Bryan and I died. Who would take care of them? If I died, would they ever know how much I loved them? They were so young; would they even remember me and the things we did? That would make me think about my mom and just get more depressed.

Worry is like meditating on negative thoughts. There was this endless record playing in my mind that said, "You suck as a mom. You're on the edge of a divorce. These kids would be better off without you. You should just kill yourself." And I was still stuck on a skipping record of guilt about my grandmother. I would have these awful nightmares about her. For years and years, it was the same theme: Grandma was waiting somewhere for me to rescue her, and I abandoned her. She was locked up in a house in one of my recurring dreams, and I couldn't get to her. "Tracy, come get me. Help me!" and I couldn't. Sometimes I was watching from the perspective of the mailbox. The mailbox was right in front of our house, and I was out there checking it, and I heard her screaming. I looked up and she was standing there screaming because she couldn't get the screen door open. She looked terrified. I tried to go inside to help her, but I couldn't get in, either.

Or she was calling and calling me and I wouldn't answer the phone. She looked so sad in my dreams, and she would say, "I'm lonesome" or "I miss you."

I tried to tell myself that she had lived a full life, and there probably wasn't anything I could have done for her, and that it was not fair to expect a sixteen-year-old to stay in that house. Who knows what would have happened? They might have killed me; I might have killed them. But the guilt ate away at me just the same. I left her. I should have taken better care of her. I wasn't there when she died.

The worst of my anxiety was in July of 1999. Elijah was

about to turn a year old. I was in the throes of a terrible panic attack, to the point where I couldn't even get out of bed. I was too embarrassed to tell anyone what was happening, so I just said I wasn't feeling well. I just stayed in bed feeling suicidal and scared.

I couldn't even get in the car to go to the grocery store; I would start hyperventilating because the devil would tell me, "If you get on the road, I'll have somebody hit you. Then you won't even have to kill yourself. I'll do it for you."

For about three weeks, I barely left the house. The thought of going anywhere made me feel physically ill—my legs cramped up and I got knots in my stomach. Bryan would get upset because he wanted to go out to dinner, and I'd make up some lame excuse for why I didn't want to go. I couldn't function, and he never knew. He thought I was just avoiding spending time with him, so his feelings were hurt.

But one night, I was in the bedroom and I couldn't breathe. I thought I was having a heart attack. Bryan came into the room, and I said, "Something is wrong with me. I don't feel good." He felt my head and told me I didn't have a fever.

"I feel like I can't breathe," I said . . . and a dam burst. I was hysterical, blurting out all these things on my mind. "There are no markers on my parents' graves. How will I ever find them? The maintenance people there cut the grass at that cemetery all the time and run over their graves and don't even know they're there. My grandmother doesn't have a headstone, either. I should have bought her a headstone! I just want to be home. I need to go home."

"What do I need to do?" he asked. "I'll put you on a flight tomorrow. Do I need to come with you?"

So I flew back to Georgia, thinking I could get my head straight there, but I didn't know what I was doing there or what was wrong with me. It only made things worse. I felt so lost and so edgy, and I wondered if there was something wrong with my hormones or my heart. I longed for my grandma to hug me, to be on the porch shelling peas and talking. I drove past her old house, and the trees were so big, and everything looked different. A lady was on the porch fixing to walk in the door when I drove up. She looked at me because I was staring, trying to see into the house. I wanted so badly to stop and ask her if I could come inside so I could go into my grandma's room just one more time. I never did, though. Eventually, I just went back home.

Bryan and I hit a breaking point where we couldn't stand each other anymore. Around October 1999, we separated. We had been married for four and a half years, and we decided it was time to walk away, so Bryan moved out.

Pretty soon, though, I realized it was the wrong decision. *I don't want my kids growing up with a stepfather,* I thought. *This isn't how it's meant to be.*

And it was a good thing that he was having the same thoughts. We both decided that we needed to try harder, instead of giving up. And we decided the way to do it was to walk more closely with God and get more involved with the church. God gave us those kids for a reason, and He put us together for a reason. That was a gift we weren't supposed to bring to the returns counter.

Putting the Lord first in our lives made a very big difference for us. We agreed to disagree about the things we had been arguing about. That didn't make all our problems go away, but it made us both more firmly planted with each other, and more determined to work through whatever came up.

We moved to a new house, partly to get a fresh start. There were too many fights in the old house, and we wanted to recognize that we were at a new place in our lives. Even though we knew we couldn't run away from anything, you can create new memories. Letting go of the Georgia mansion was symbolic for me. Sometimes, the things you imagine to be so magnificent as a child don't turn out to be so great. It just wasn't me at all, and we were ready to build something that was going to better reflect our real style and who we were now. So we moved into this big, beautiful house with a special prayer room with stained-glass windows, and we hired a painter to paint angels in the room. Without knowing it, the painter painted one of the angels with a face very similar to my grandmother's.

It seems to be there as a constant reminder that our prosperity is from the Lord.

The house became an interesting conglomerate of high culture, crayon drawings, photographs everywhere, murals, and crosses. So now I had the most beautiful house I had ever seen, and it was exactly what I had envisioned.

I saw a few different psychiatrists and therapists at different points, trying to talk through everything from my parents' deaths to the abuse I went through to my marital troubles. One therapist told me, "You really need to be angry with your grandmother, because she made some bad choices."

At first, I thought this was really obnoxious advice. *Who are you to judge her? Who are you to tell me how to feel about the woman who raised me?* I thought. But I was still waking up in cold sweats with these guilt-ridden nightmares and thoughts about all the ways I'd let her down.

Even though I didn't like what the therapist had said because I thought it was disrespectful, the words played around in my head over the days and weeks to come. She wasn't perfect. I had always known that she was wrong to consistently choose her sons over us, to let them get away with the abusive and humiliating behavior that was their daily routine.

So maybe I could be mad. A little.

Maybe it was okay to let go of a little of that guilt, to acknowledge that it was okay for me to leave the situation because my grandmother had made the bad decision to put me in danger in that house. I could still love her and remember all the good things about her, but I could also feel angry that she handled things so badly and didn't pro-tect me the way she should have.

When I told a psychiatrist about the anxiety I was having, he told me I had panic attacks and prescribed Xanax. I had to learn to work through the attacks, too, though, not just rely on the pills. When I'm getting very anxious, I have to stop and think to myself, *Is this worth the energy you're putting into this? There are so many things to put time and effort into. Is this important?* Usually, the answer is no.

My definition of being a good mother changed, too. It took me time to realize that if I didn't get the boys to bed exactly at 9:00, or have their lunch ready at noon, or get them into a bath every night, life would go on. Being present not just for them, but for myself, was important. The things that they really wanted from me were the things I take joy in: tucking them in at night, praying with them, baking cookies after school, cuddling up on the couch.

Because of my anxieties and fears about inadequacy as a mom, I was obsessive for a long time about silly things. I would go check on the boys seven or eight times a night to make sure their covers hadn't fallen off. But you know what? If they were cold, they could pull their covers up themselves.

I think I became a better mom once I let myself take a breath and remembered that I was allowed to experience joy in motherhood. I love it when they have friends sleep over and I can put popcorn in bowls and set up sleeping bags and watch them make memories together. The next morning, I love making breakfast for them and all their friends and feeling like a short-order cook at Waffle House.

The process was gradual, and I never thought it would happen the way other parents say it does. When Jacob was a toddler and his pacifier fell out onto the floor, I'd rush over to wash and sterilize it before I would let it near his lips. When Elijah did the same thing, I'd just brush the dog hair off it, lick it, and hand it back. Other moms would tell me that's how it goes, and when I just had Jacob, I would self-righteously think, *No, you might have turned into a slacker, but that'll never be me.* I don't think there's a script for being a good mom, and at one point I thought there was.

The boys grew up with Jesus, like a fifth member of our family. They had "baby Bibles" since birth and went to church with us, and just like with any storybook, I'd read them stories about Jesus. But I'd tell them that these stories were real, not like the other picture books. I wanted them to know that Jesus was not this untouchable concept, this far-away mythical being, so we always talked about Him like He was a person right there in the house with us. And lots of times, we felt Him there, too.

When we would pray in their bedroom, we could feel the presence of the Lord. "How awesome that He would take the time to come here and be with us when we pray," I'd tell them. They learned that you didn't have to get dressed up when Jesus came to visit, that He wanted to hang out with you just as you are. I told them that Jesus loved everybody and didn't walk around judging people, and that He taught that it wasn't our place to judge how people lived their lives.

Elijah has seemed to have many spiritual challenges already in his short life. He really didn't speak until he was three years old, and then it came out all mixed up and garbled. We got him into speech therapy, and it was heartbreaking to watch him struggle to communicate. It was also hard to compare the boys, because when Jacob started speaking, he spoke in full sentences immediately. His first words were "Pass me the red apple." So I knew something was wrong here, but I didn't know what. I worried that he had a disability that would stay with him, something that might block his ability to communicate with the world.

And so I laid my body across his one night, weeping and praying, "God, please help him. I don't even know what we're up against. I don't know what to pray for." It felt so desperate, not knowing what was wrong or how to fix it. And God said to me, "The devil is trying to steal his tongue."

"Steal his tongue? Why would he want his tongue?"

"He's trying to steal his tongue because of all the good things Elijah is going to say for me."

God explained that the devil knew that if Elijah were self-conscious about his speech, he'd be afraid to go and speak out about how awesome God is. It made sense to me, and I prayed to keep the devil away from my son. Soon, his speech became clearer and clearer, and today, he talks up a storm without any problems.

He grew into a boy who oozes charisma—wherever we go on vacation, people in the hotel or on the beach will ask me where Elijah is, or come over to tell me how great he is. Like me, he loves to be the center of attention, and he's quick-witted and street-smart, as opposed to Jacob's book-smarts. They're opposites in many ways. Jacob is the serious one, the one who could sit all day in his room and read a book and be perfectly content. He's also the "mad genius" type, who always sees the big picture, but details are not important to him. His room can be a mess and it doesn't bother him; as long as he can find his computer and has a place for his books, he's good. And his shoes are always untied.

Jacob wants to be the President of the United States when he grows up. I know lots of kids say that, but he's serious, and we take him seriously. He recently read a book about personality types and was delighted to find that he has the same personality type as Winston Churchill and George W. Bush.

"Mr. President, when you're in the White House, you're going to have to tie your shoes," Elijah told him.

Jacob looked at him and said, "Have you ever seen George Bush in shoes that lace up?"

Mind you, Elijah's shoes are lined up in his closet according to color. He's more orderly and practical, whereas Jacob is the idea factory who is always thinking big. The first time Jacob took a skiing lesson, he wanted to go straight to the double black diamond trails instead of bothering with the bunny slopes. They're both sensitive, but Jacob cries at movies like *Radio*, the story where Cuba Gooding, Jr. plays a mentally disabled athlete shunned by the community.

He also cries sometimes about his desire to protect his brother. The other day, he told me he had a bad dream and was really upset. "Tell me," I said.

"We were at the beach, and Elijah got taken by a wave, and I couldn't make it to save him," he said. "The wave had a face—two eyes and a smile as it took him under. I swam sixty feet and I couldn't hold my breath anymore. I couldn't save him and he died." His face flooded with tears.

"Don't worry," I said. "You know your dad and I are always with you at the beach. Your dad is like David Hasselhoff in *Baywatch*, and he can run down that beach and save you in no time flat." I was trying to make him smile, but it didn't work.

"It was the worst feeling I ever had," he said, choking back sobs.

I knew the dream was symbolic of all the responsibility he feels to protect his little brother, a responsibility that carries over to the protection of lots of other kids, too. When we went to the roller skating rink recently, there was a disabled boy and his mom slowly moving around the rink, and I pointed him out to Jacob. Right away, he skated over and began talking to the boy, encouraging him. "You're such a good skater! You're doing a great job!" and skating by his side all around the rink so no one would bump into him or bother him.

The boy's mother came over to me later and told me I had the nicest son she'd ever met. I hope that we have taught them well by example, but the truth is that my boys do these things naturally. It's what's in their hearts and always has been. I never had to teach them not to make fun of others. I never had to tell them to be "nice" to kids who are different. They're the ones who would come home and tell me about all the great things someone did in class that day, and I'd later find out that the kid was handicapped. It was like the boys skipped right past the part where you need to teach them tolerance and acceptance and went straight to the enlightened part where they decided to be champions of the underdogs and friends of the friendless.

To do that, you need to have a certain self-confidence, which both of them have. But Elijah faced another spiritual challenge in 2005 when he played football. Every Saturday, his dad and I would go watch him play, and when he was on the field he didn't even look like our kid. He was so self-conscious and nervous, shrinking down into nothing. It drove me crazy because I knew that wasn't his personality. I knew it had to be a spiritual problem, so I kept praying, "Lord, I know the devil is trying to make him insecure again, to sabotage him and ruin his confidence. Help him be what you've called him to be."

"Tracy, it's just a football game," Bryan would say. "You're overreacting."

But to me, it wasn't just a football game. It was a battle

I was watching in progress. My son was unsure of every move he made, not at all like his normal self. And if he learned to shrink back in football, he might learn to shrink back in other areas of life, too, to lose his footing and stop trusting his instincts.

So I stayed in his room and prayed after Elijah went to sleep one night, "God, give him the confidence of David when he battled Goliath." I heard footsteps across the carpet, so I opened my eyes to see Bryan come into the room. God said, "Why are you looking at him when you're talking to me?" So I closed my eyes again and kept praying. I felt Bryan standing beside me, but he walked out before I finished. When I got back to bed, Bryan was already asleep.

The next morning, I said, "That was so sweet that you came in and stood with me when I was praying for Elijah."

"I don't know what you're talking about," he said. "I never got up last night."

I knew then that it was Jesus standing beside me during my prayer, bolstering me as I asked Him to bolster my son.

—— *Eight* ——

WE ALWAYS TITHED AND ALWAYS DONATED GEN-
erously because it was the right thing to do, not because we
wanted to look important. But I remember the first time I
felt called to do something on a larger scale. Jacob was a
baby then, and Bryan and I were sitting in the back of this
big church. The pastor announced that they were looking
to buy some land in another country, and they had an
opportunity to buy a plot for a few thousand dollars. It was
a great deal. He didn't say he was looking for donations
toward the land, but he said he was praying to find out what
the church was meant to do with this land, and asked us to
pray about it, too.

I thought to myself, *God wants me to buy this.* I turned to
Bryan and said, "I think we're meant to buy this land for
the church."

He gave me a look that said, "I trust you with this, you
don't even need to ask." And I went to the pastor with a

check in hand for the full amount. The pastor didn't know us at the time, and is not the type to chase after the church's big contributors and put them on display or fawn over them, which I was happy about. In church, he just said that a "generous couple" had bought the land for the church, and I got to feel good about it without having to stand up and wave.

The church is involved with many outreach projects, though, and we had forgotten where the land was located. Later, the church asked for volunteers to fly to Nicaragua to build an orphanage, a school, and a church. Bryan went. He knew he could have just written a check. Sometimes, when you have money, it's easy to just write checks and feel like you're doing enough. But Bryan decided it would be more of a sacrifice for him to actually be there, to take time away from the office and put on work boots and help them dig and build the plumbing. He wouldn't let me come because he was afraid I'd bring home eighteen children, though!

We didn't make the association that this was being built on our gift to the church until the pastor announced afterwards that this new orphanage, school, and church would not exist without the donation from the couple who had bought the land.

"Wait, *we* bought that land!" I said to Bryan. How exciting it was to know it had gone to such great use. We would go on to help build an orphanage in Brazil, too.

What I've found very rewarding, and what I've passed on to my children, is to make charity an everyday act, something that gets incorporated into our lives as normally as eating and sleeping. The big donations are exhilarating, but the small acts can be just as meaningful. When we bought that land, a few thousand dollars was big money to us. Now we get to do things on an even bigger scale when there's need.

Through a friend in church, we met Larry Jones from Feed the Children. Immediately, we connected with him because of his honesty. This is a guy who really does live his mission. He doesn't take a big salary, he still drives a truck, and he and his wife don't live extravagant lives. They are foot soldiers for God, going wherever there are children in need and finding a way to help. Their goal is to make sure no child ever goes hungry. One of the coolest things about Larry is that even with all the thousands of children he's helped, he still really wants to meet every child and every family he helps, to talk to them and find out who they are. And he remembers them, even years later and thousands of other kids in between. We have worked closely with Feed the Children, and truly believe in what they do.

So after Hurricane Katrina, it was a thrill to be able to tell Larry that he could send out more trucks, because we were donating enough money to buy the fuel to make sure he could get plenty more food and relief supplies to the disaster area. Larry invited my family to go on one of the trips to the Gulf Coast. Bryan wasn't able to go because he had meetings, but we decided it would be good for the boys and me to be there. For this trip, the National Basketball

Association had teamed up with Feed the Children to deliver supplies. Of course, Jacob and Elijah were thrilled to find that out.

We were in a convoy of eighteen-wheelers, vans, and buses that headed up the Gulf Coast starting in Jackson, Mississippi, and ending in Gulfport, Mississippi. Along the way, we made stops to hand out food and supplies such as water, soap, baby formula, tissues, and diapers to people in need. It still felt like the middle of summer even though it wasn't. The boys helped get the boxes off the trucks. I knew the people were grateful, and you could see how excited they were that the guys they watched on television cared enough to come help them. I was just as proud of my kids, to see them trying to do their part.

Jacob and Elijah rode on the bus with the players. Riding in an SUV behind the bus, I laughed to myself. There was no telling what they were saying or doing on that bus, but I knew they were having a blast.

When we arrived in Gulfport, it was lunch time. Some sweet local people had set up a tent with picnic tables and were cooking for everyone, locals and volunteers alike. It was still mostly a ghost town because we were there right after the hurricanes. There was also a makeshift medical trailer. The seriousness of the situation set in when we were stepping over stagnant water, flies everywhere, and we were all told we needed to get shots to protect us from whatever was in that water.

We went to a local church where people were waiting to help unload the truck. There were some soldiers there who had just come from Iraq; they had been brought in specifically to help. While the NBA guys were handing out the supplies, Jacob and Elijah spotted the soldiers and went over and started up a conversation. I could see they were both completely enamored.

I walked over in time to hear one of the soldiers say to Jacob, "It must be pretty cool to get to hang out with all those NBA guys."

Jacob smiled and said, "They're cool and everything, but I think you're much cooler. You're really a hero."

Jacob and Elijah followed those servicemen around, wanting to know what every stripe and pin on their uniforms meant, wanting to talk about their experiences. Completely against protocol, by the end of the trip, the soldiers each took a pin off their uniforms and gave them to the boys.

"Just when I was feeling like nobody cared, to have a little boy come over and say that to me is really amazing," one of them said to me.

Our last stop was at the beach where the hurricane had actually come in. We had special permission to go there with Feed the Children, so we got through the barricades and roadblocks to film some footage. It was so sad to see the destruction—tops of hotels and casinos that had been completely ripped off were sitting on top of other four- or five-story buildings crushed into the ground.

Getting out and walking around, no one knew quite what to say. The stench in the air was nauseating. While we tried to take it all in, Elijah said, "Right now, it doesn't matter who you are—NBA player or not—this is so sad to see." It was so still. We knew to be careful, and had been warned about safety protocol. We were told there were still bodies under some of the debris, and you could sense that.

On the way home, I asked the boys what they would remember from the trip. Elijah said he would never forget how sad the people looked and how sad it must have been to stand in line for something as simple as toilet paper and food. Jacob said he would never forget the smell on the beach. "That was the smell of death, Mom," he said, and he was right. It's not something you ever forget.

Even though the situations are depressing and shocking sometimes, I find it very fulfilling to be there to help out how I can. I love to meet people and talk to them and hear their hearts. I have friends who say it's cute the way I'll do little things, like put together bags of clothes, hair products, and knee-highs for the elderly people who were affected by the hurricanes, but I don't think it's cute. My grandmother would get very out of sorts when she didn't have her knee-high stockings, and I imagined that it would be a comfort for these women to have the things they were used to, not just the basic supplies that everyone else would have thought of.

The "little things" can mean a lot to people, and I like that God uses me to show people He hasn't forgotten them, that He still cares. And whether you have a billion dollars or twenty dollars, there are things you can always do to help other people in need. Even when you have nothing, you can always pray for people and talk to them when they need someone to listen and hold their hands when they're scared or alone. It costs nothing to give people hope.

In the nonprofit world, there are usually two types of people who get involved—one is the kind who donate their money, and the other is the kind who donate their time. But both are important to me. It's sometimes frustrating to know that society expects me to just be one or the other. I'm expected to write a check and be on the board and on the committees and go to tea parties and have my picture in the paper. But you know what? I don't want to be on the board or the committee, and I don't need special acknowledgment for what I do. What I have comes from God, and He's the one who deserves the credit. What's more important to me than my own public validation is to know that I'm doing right with what God provides, to know that we're pleasing him by helping others.

So I asked Larry, "Am I supposed to pick between those worlds?"

"No," he said. "I think God will give you a balance."

And I think He does. My family and I have helped fund spa days for battered women, a luncheon for single mothers on Mother's Day, and lots of other things. Whenever I invite people over to my house, they know I have some kind of ulterior motive—there's always something I'm trying to set up or a project I want their help with. At Bryan's fortieth birthday party, we asked for donations to Feed the Children instead of gifts. At a Christmas party, I asked people to bring sleeping bags and clothes that we could give to homeless people.

People sometimes make comments about giving money to homeless people—"Oh, they're just going to use it to buy beer!" or "He's just scamming you." And sometimes they're surely right, but that's not my business. If I have twenty dollars in my pocket and I see a homeless person, I will give away my twenty dollars. Once it's out of my hands, my part of the job is over. What the person decides to do with it is not my business. I don't have the right to judge how the person uses the money, a lesson I've tried to pass on to my kids. If they're going to buy beer, well, I've been around alcoholics. I know what addiction is like, and what DTs look like, and if that's what it takes to get them through the day, that's their business. I'm not about to point my nose in the air and tell people to sober up so they can have clearer vision of life on the street.

We give with a glad heart, just as we do whenever we give to any charity. It's hard to know just where your money is going to end up, or whether or not a charity is crooked. But once the donation has left your hands, you've honored God with your intentions. It's up to the recipient to do the same, or not.

One day we were driving to a Mavericks game, and there

was a dirty homeless man standing at an intersection with a sign that said, "Will work for food."

"Sure," Bryan muttered under his breath. "I try to hire people every day . . . I always need people to work. He doesn't really want to work."

Something came over me and I really flew off the handle.

"Would you hire him looking like *that*?"

"No," Bryan said.

"He can't just go anywhere and shower and shave and get new clothes! You want to think he's just lazy, but how is he supposed to get a job and get a new start when he looks like that? No one's going to hire him!"

Bryan grew up in Dallas, and he had become jaded because there were always homeless people around the streets. The same thing happens to people in New York, Chicago, Los Angeles . . . all the big cities. You forget, maybe, that these people are still human and still God's children, no matter what turns their lives have taken.

I reminded Bryan and the kids—who were sitting in the back seat in stunned silence—about how my father's father had died homeless on the streets, alone, and how he certainly didn't choose that destiny. He made bad choices, but that isn't what he wanted.

"That man on the street could be Jesus. At the least, he's somebody's son. He was Elijah's age once, and he had dreams and goals. He didn't want to end up a crackhead on the street."

By that time, we had driven past the homeless man, so Bryan swung the car around and drove back to him and gave the man some money. It changed his heart.

That winter, we started a project called "At Least Somebody's Son." We went to Costco and bought about fifty sleeping bags, socks, gloves, hats, flannel shirts, and duffel bags. We wanted to get jackets, but we were trying to think practically: The whole package was supposed to roll up into the sleeping bag and fit into the duffel bag so the recipients could carry it around from place to place.

Then we bought McDonald's gift cards, to give the homeless people a chance to sit inside and get some coffee and something to eat. Elijah suggested gift certificates to 7-Eleven, too, so we got those. Then we put cash into envelopes to include, too.

We laid everything out all over the living room and prayed over it.

Then we loaded it all up into the car, and on Christmas Eve we drove to where there weren't any shelters, just homeless people on the street. When we saw someone, we'd stop the car and roll down the window and hand out a bag and say, "God bless you." You meet a lot of interesting people that way. Sometimes, Bryan would have to get out and bring the bag over to someone who couldn't walk, or who was passed out on the sidewalk. Sometimes, people would just snatch the bag out of our hands and walk away without saying anything. That's okay; you never really know what's going on in someone's head.

But other people make you really glad you took the time to bother. One in particular really touched me.

"Excuse me, sir, I have something for you," I called out to a man.

He looked at us suspiciously for a moment, then tentatively came closer. "A lot of times, people spit at me from the car," he said.

"Well, we won't be doing any spitting," I assured him. "We just came here to bless you and to tell you that God loves you and we love you, and we hope that this helps."

He began crying and told us that the night before, he had gotten beaten up and all of his stuff was stolen. I don't think it was any coincidence that God brought us to him that night.

Seeing women on the streets bothered Bryan more than seeing men did. One woman looked like me. She couldn't look him in the eye. You just never know what circumstances led them to where they are. There are former CEOs of companies and newspaper editors who are now homeless. Jacob was very bothered when we encountered an old man who told us he was a World War II veteran. He smelled of alcohol and was leaning up against a building when we approached him.

"Mom, he served our country and now he's homeless," Jacob said later.

After that, I started keeping McDonald's cards and extra cash in my car console, so whenever we encountered homeless people, we'd have something to give. And I tried to think about the things they'd need that they probably couldn't buy for themselves, like deodorant, toothpaste, and feminine products. Your body doesn't know when you're homeless; it still functions just the same as when you have a roof over your head and a closet full of drug store items. I knew what it felt like not to have a home.

I've learned to take advantage of the gifts that God has given me and to use them for His benefit. Not just money, but connections, the ability to talk to people, the ability to get people's attention. I know that having expensive jewelry and fancy cars gets people's attention, and I know it's a superficial reason for them to pay attention—but it works. You can function in social circles that you wouldn't otherwise gain entrance to. People think you must know the secrets of life if you're rich and attractive, so I tell them: It's all about the Lord. And He wants us to help everyone who needs help.

I am still simple about a lot of things, in a world that's not so simple. I just genuinely care about people, and it makes me sad to know that there are kids who will go to sleep hungry tonight and grandparents struggling to get by. I'm motivated by the memories of my own family and how much they struggled.

I tell my kids that integrity is not what you do when people are looking, but when people aren't looking. I don't need to have a dozen people watch me make phone calls on behalf of a couple down on their luck in need of an apartment, and tell me, "Oh, she's going to heaven for that."

With many things I've done, I'll never get a thank you, and that's okay. God already knows my heart, whether other people notice or not.

I believe the reason God has brought me through so many things and blessed me with so much is so I can help other people. Ultimately in life, my biggest concern is that one day I will stand before the Lord and he will ask me whether I did all I could have done with what I was given. I want to be able to say, "I did everything I could do." In response, I want Him to say, "You did a great job." I don't want Him to say, "You didn't do half of what you could have done."

To be really effective at helping others, though, you can't let yourself break down in the process. And that's why God knew, even in the midst of helping so many people, that it was time for me to back up and finish taking care of myself. This time, He told me, He wasn't going to carry me through it. I was going to have to find my own way to walk through those places in my mind I never wanted to go again.

— *Nine* —

THE MIGRAINES WERE OUT OF CONTROL. IT WAS to the point where the boys knew just how to react because they were so used to seeing me in pain.

I'd be in bed sick, throwing up from these headaches, and I hated that my kids would see me this way, weak and pitiful. My fear was that they would hurt for me the way I used to hurt for my mom. I never wanted them to feel like caregivers.

Some days, I was so ill from the headaches that other people would have to pick them up from school. Then I'd just lie there miserably, imagining their disappointment when someone other than me picked them up. I knew what it felt like to wish your mom wasn't sick all the time. *Why does it have to be my mom who's always in bed and feeling awful? Why not someone else?*

I saw a lot of myself in Elijah—the cold rags and glasses of water he would bring me, pulling the covers back on my bed—it was all too familiar.

I don't think anyone knew how often and how badly I was suffering, or what I was doing about it.

I battled the migraines daily, and so much of my life was centered on trying to keep them at bay. Certain things would trigger them every time: skipping meals, lack of caffeine, particular smells. It's funny how smells can bring you right back to other places in time. The smell of fried foods, especially pork chops, would give me an instant headache. My grandmother always fried pork chops when she was trying to sober up my uncles. If I smelled strong floral perfume, the same thing happened. My mom used to wear that kind of perfume.

Any sort of stress or pressure would put me in danger. Some days I actually wound up in the emergency room, and doctors would have to give me intravenous fluids.

So I convinced myself that it was okay to take pain pills several times a day. After all, I was taking them as the doctor prescribed, not taking them to get high, and I was taking them for a legitimate reason: constant migraines. In addition, I was taking Valium for anxiety.

My purse was like my own personal traveling pharmacy. I carried around bottles and bottles of pills and never thought anything much of it. It was something I had seen my whole life. My grandmother had medication that she carried around in her purse. No matter what the problem, there was a purse somewhere in the house that had something in it to make you feel better. It was fairly innocent, though, like, "Oh, you have a toothache? Here's some pain medication for that."

When my uncles were drunk and I had to go to school the next day, my grandma would sometimes give me a half of a pill "to help me rest." It was a Valium. I didn't know that then, but I know it now. I realize that, even then, I was being taught not to deal with things. She was only doing what she thought was right.

I may not have had much else in my purse, but I never left home without those pills. I never could tell when a migraine was going to strike. It was a security blanket for me. I would often joke about taking them. But the truth was that I couldn't be without them.

But it was the kitchen drawer that got me "caught." One day, Bryan was looking in a drawer for something, and he came across some empty pill bottles and asked me about them.

"What's all this?" he asked. "You take all these?"

"You know . . ." I stammered. "They're for my migraines."

"How many are you taking a day?"

"I don't know."

Even as the words came out, they felt shameful. The tears flooded my cheeks; I felt like I'd been caught doing something naughty. But I didn't know how I was supposed to live without them.

Bryan is the kind of guy who doesn't even take aspirin. Seeing a bunch of empty medicine bottles didn't mean anything to me, but it horrified him. And maybe part of me knew that. I'm not sure why I was keeping all those empty bottles around, in the middle of the kitchen. On some subconscious level, maybe I wanted him to see. How else was I going to get up the nerve to say I needed help? He went online and researched opiate painkiller addiction, and it terrified him. He was horrified that I was going to die from an overdose or liver disease.

Bryan told me I needed to get help, and I knew he was right. If I was going to come off these pain medications, two things were going to have to happen: First of all, I'd have to figure out what was causing all these migraines in the first place and deal with that, and second, I'd have to get some help with the withdrawal symptoms I knew I would have. Legal or illegal, substance addiction is the same. You go through detox, which can make you very sick, especially if you try to do it without a doctor's supervision.

We talked it through and decided that the right thing was for me to go into a rehab program, where I could get both medical and psychological support. I searched around for facilities online. The first one I contacted felt wrong—it sounded like a jail. They had so many rules about what you could and couldn't bring, and the person I spoke to was cold. So I kept looking, and I found one that looked promising. Their Web site described their approach, which was very focused on individual and group therapy. Every client would see ten different therapists a week, and the setting was like a beautiful beachfront resort. You don't have to cut yourself off from your family (cell phones were allowed), there wasn't a whole list of things you can't bring, no one locks you in, and doctors and nurses are on duty all the time. Their goal was to find and treat the underlying causes of addiction, not just fix the addiction itself.

Well, that sounded like what I was looking for. I didn't just want to come off the medication; I wanted to find real healing. I had always dealt with the various traumas in my life as best as I could at the time, then tried to bury them and move on with my life. It was very hard for me to dredge up old memories.

Even some of the most important people in my life knew only the barebones version of what happened to me growing up. I could talk about the Cliff's Notes version— my parents died, I lived with my grandmother in the Projects, I got addicted to drugs—but the details are what got me. I didn't like to put myself in positions where people might ask too many questions, and then I'd have to actually go back to that place in my mind and think about the way my mom looked before she died and the cockroaches in the dishrags and the smell of my uncle's bedroom.

Even though I had gone for some counseling, the therapists always recommended medication for me to deal with my problems. Maybe this place was different. I felt like I had a lot of unfinished business to deal with, and maybe going away for a few weeks in an intensive program like this would be the right thing. So I scheduled my stay right away, before I had much time to reconsider. Then the fear set in.

Mostly, I was freaked out about leaving my family. The rehab center suggests that you stay for at least a month, and I didn't know if I was going to be able to be without my kids and my husband for that long. Plus, how was he going to handle taking care of them like I did? Was he going to make them breakfast every day and pick them up from school and help make costumes for the school play like I did? Was he going to do a good job of tucking them in and praying over them and kissing them goodnight? Was I going to be able to sleep without seeing their faces?

As the second thoughts kicked in, they were the ones who talked me back into it. We had told the kids that this was a nice place, not like a hospital. It was like a house with doctors and therapists, and they would help me find out why I was having headaches and learn a more natural way to deal with them.

"It's just a month," Jacob said, "But it could make you feel better the rest of your life. No more headaches."

The first day they put me in a big room with a sweet young roommate, who I could immediately see as somebody's daughter who had just made some bad choices. She could tell I didn't really want to talk, so she left me alone. I just sat there hating myself for being there and feeling like a bad mom and feeling the weight of my husband's disappointment. How had I gone and screwed it up again? I went to bed in tears and hoped I was doing the right thing.

In the morning, I went to the kitchen for breakfast and ran into a very aggressive woman who was also there for treatment.

"So, what are you here for?" she asked.

"Huh?"

"What did you do? Why are you here?"

"Oh. Pain pills," I said, and tried to drop the conversation.

"How many were you taking?"

"I don't know. Maybe ten a day."

"That's nothing. I was taking thirty-five a day. *And* drinking all day on top of it, too."

I didn't say anything. I wasn't aware we were having a contest. I just tried to get through the day, acting as friendly as I could even though I just wanted to curl up in bed by myself and shut out the world.

The first week was rough. Really rough. For the first time in my life, I felt like I had lost myself. I felt like I didn't have legs to stand on. My energy was gone, and I was crippled. As much as I asked God to intervene and make this easier for me, this time He wouldn't.

"Lord, I'm done," I said. "Why are you letting all of this happen to me? Where are you? Why do I have to be here? I've witnessed for you, I've given you the glory in my life . . . why do I have to go through this?"

It's funny to think about it now, how stupid it was for me

to sit there thinking about what I had done for God, when it could never compare to what He had done for me. How many times had he picked me up by my britches, dusted me off, and made my life easier?

"I've carried you so many times. You've got to walk this one out," He told me.

He'd still be there with me, but He wasn't going to do it for me and just miraculously take away my withdrawal. Maybe I couldn't have handled it then, but this was almost like God telling me that He knew I was ready for this, that I could do it. I had to do it.

Like a spoiled child, I didn't like hearing that. I was very used to God fixing things for me. Even with all the tough things I went through in life, I still could pray and know my prayers would be answered. Sometimes instantly. This time was different.

There's a saying: "God protects fools and babies." I wasn't a fool or a baby anymore, and it was time for me to do the work. It felt like spiritual warfare, like I was fighting for my life. All around me were people who had totally different beliefs than mine, and in some cases, they were trying to make me feel very stupid for my beliefs. There were Buddhist and Hindu symbols on the walls and shelves, and a spiritual counselor who seemed to believe in New Age ideas, but there were no crosses or other signs of Christianity.

Normally, this would not have bothered me. After all, I

feel that if you truly stand for something, and you know what you stand for, you aren't intimidated by others' beliefs and ideas. I don't have to have all the paraphernalia to know who my God is, nor do I need to let others know my beliefs. My heart and actions should speak louder than any plaque or bumper sticker. But in this case, I was looking for anything familiar. I missed Bryan, the boys, and my home, and I was looking for something to remind me of them, to feel connected to them.

For the first week coming off the pills, I was working so hard just to stand upright that I didn't have the energy to argue about it. But I prayed about it, wondering what I was doing in a place where there were tarot cards and crystals in place of Scripture. It gave me the creeps, like I was in a bad dream. It all felt very one-sided to me. In one sense, this is why rehab can be so effective. But I didn't like the idea that I check in as one person and check out as another, not just dropping the pills but dropping my beliefs too.

When you're first going through detox, you're not required to attend all the therapy sessions at this particular center. You have the option of staying in your room if you're feeling really bad, which I was. Detox was hard for me, and the doctor at the rehab center said it was actually worse because I wasn't taking the medicine in order to get high.

"You would have been better off if you were taking five or six at a time and getting a buzz off them instead of taking them every four hours as they were prescribed," he said in a teasing way, but the sentiment was true. He said it was harder for my body to get rid of the drug because it was used to having it so regularly.

You have got to be kidding me, I thought.

It was there I started thinking about Jonah and his dumb choices. God had called Jonah to go to Nineveh and preach against the sins he saw there, but Jonah decided to run away and get on a ship and flee to a different city. Then came a terrible storm, and the ship was about to break. The men knew it was Jonah who had brought them the trouble, so they threw him overboard (hey, he volunteered), which is when he got swallowed by a whale (or, as my son Jacob would correct me, a grouper) and lived in its belly for three days. I'm pretty sure he sat there for those three days thinking, *Man, I wish I had just done what God told me to do in the first place.* If he had just gone to Nineveh, he could have avoided the whole fish thing!

Yeah, Tracy, if you had just come off those darn pills years ago, you wouldn't need to be stuck here holding onto the walls in rehab.

Sure, if you want to make me admit it, I think I was scared to become what I was called to be. It's a lot of responsibility living up to God's plans for you. Lots of people are scared and spend their lives running away from being who God calls them to be. The pills were just another weight holding me back. As long as I kept taking them, I was always going to be in this vicious cycle of pain and lack of energy and avoidance where I'd stay stagnant and never grow past my problems.

Going to rehab was like saying to God, "Okay, I'm not running away anymore." But announcing that didn't make it easy. My head swam, my stomach buckled, and everything hurt. It felt like the flu, with severe abdominal cramps and aches all over, with depression and anxiety thrown in as extra bonuses. To get through it I had to keep reminding myself that this was just a detour. It wasn't going to last forever, and something good was going to come of it.

That's hard to remember when you have a seven-year-old and a ten-year-old trying to act like they're fine on the other end of the phone. Every morning, they would call on Elijah's way to school, and I would usually talk to Jacob at lunchtime. He was being homeschooled. I had bought a book that I thought Jacob would like, and I read it on the phone to him every day, to try to keep some consistency, because we read together a lot at home. He would call and say, "Can we read?" and I would try not to cry, even though it ripped out my heart.

For Elijah, we had gone to Build-a-Bear before I left and made a bunny and a chick, as early Easter presents. He kept one, and I brought the other with me, to remind us of each other. I told him that when he went to sleep, he should hug the chick and know that I was thinking about him and I would do the same thing with the bunny.

Bryan and the boys sent me roses, so I had flowers all

over the room, and I lit candles to make it feel more like home. My roommate was moved to another room after just a day or two, so I had this whole huge suite to myself, with two king beds. We joked that I had the hotel suite.

At the rehab facility, they suggest that you start attending at least the group sessions as soon as you feel able so that you can hit the ground running, and pretty soon, you get a daily schedule tacked up to the bulletin board in the mornings telling you exactly where you need to be and when. Everyone has different schedules, written out on paper every day to tell you when you need to be in sessions, when to go to lunch, when you have free time, everything. My schedule included spiritual counseling that I didn't agree with and lectures on metaphysics.

"Why do I have to go to these things I don't believe in?" I asked a staff member. "I'm paying to be here. It should be my choice."

"The rules are the rules," he said. "You have to follow the schedule."

I didn't agree with him. I understood why the therapy sessions were mandatory. But I thought that spiritual counseling should be a personal choice and that several options should be available for consideration. *How would a metaphysics lecture help me recover?* I wondered.

With the majority of my detox over I was feeling much clearer, and I saw how vulnerable all of us were. For the most part, everyone coming in there felt ashamed, embarrassed and weak. When you are in that state of mind, it is easy to be swayed. Being told something over and over by an authority figure, well, it reminded me of the Wizard of Oz. Dorothy only wanted to go home, and she was desperate. The great Wizard was powerful and all-knowing. But when she saw what was behind the curtain, she realized it was all a fraud, that she had the ability in herself to get back home. Not everyone at the clinic could see behind the curtain, though, and I was concerned.

I called Bryan and talked to him about it. I had good reports to share about the quality of the therapists who were disarming and let you be yourself no matter what you believed. But I complained about the mandatory lectures and spiritual counseling that I felt was taking advantage of people in a highly vulnerable state. I recalled the clinic's information brochure, which boasted they had a library filled with books. But the entire collection hammered the same views as the lectures. I started to get really worked up, but Bryan calmed me down and urged me to go to the counseling session but to make it on my own terms.

The paraphernalia was the first thing that needed to go. For me, "spiritual counseling" involved spending time with the Lord, and I knew he didn't need any props to show up! I didn't want there to be any tarot cards in sight! God doesn't need any gimmicks to perform. I can hear from God without any props. I told the counselor this and asked that we take our meetings outside in the fresh air. She agreed, and we sat on a bench outside in the sun and just talked. I felt that I was supposed to ask about her life. We ended up getting along just fine. It's much easier to see someone's heart in the sunlight.

For the metaphysics lectures, I took my Bible. I wasn't rude or disrespectful to the speaker. But when something was said that I didn't believe in, I would write down what I believed. One of the guys in my group came up to me and said that he saw me taking notes and knew that I didn't want to forget any of the valuable insight. We both laughed and walked out.

I was forming fast friendships with many people there, and not the kinds of people I expected to meet in rehab. We were such a funny cross-section of life, from teenagers to business professionals. There were twenty eight of us in total, moms and dads, sons and daughters. We all ate breakfast, lunch, and dinner together in the main house, and we'd hang out together and watch movies. The view from the back of the house looked out across to the Pacific Ocean.

"I'm going to treat you to lunch today," one of my new friends said.

"That is so sweet!" I said back, and he disappeared with a grin.

Another friend at the table laughed at me and said, "Tracy, think about this for a minute. Have you paid for any meals here?"

"Oh. Hey!"

The chef made us amazing food, and he was just as amazing. He cared so much about the people who came through, and he would tell all of us every day, "You look great!" In the beginning, I told him he was full of it. By the end, I said, "I'm starting to believe you." All our needs were cared for. Even massages were included.

The experience was a huge blessing. The therapists didn't make me feel bad, or try to find blame, or make me feel like a helpless addict. That was the right approach for me, because if they had tried to make me feel any more ashamed of myself than I already felt, I probably would have relapsed the moment I got off the plane.

Instead, they gave me a very safe place to open up and explore the feelings I had been burying for so many years. Most of us spend our whole lives trying to hurry up and get past bad things and not think about them, when there's a part of us that needs to grieve and be sad.

For so long, I felt like emotion was a weakness. Other people had their problems, too; what was so special about my problems? There were always people who had it worse than I did. I was taught by example in my childhood that you aren't supposed to make a big deal of your problems, and that you should just be grateful and go on. So much of what triggered my headaches were these memories and fears skulking around in my brain.

When I first went into therapy, I was very guarded. I had

already decided that I was not going to fall apart in front of these people. But that went out the window fast.

My therapist at a one-on-one session told me, "I want you to go back and picture yourself at age seven, and talk to little Tracy."

What a bunch of psycho-nonsense! I thought. *Here we go with the inner child . . .*

But I went along with it, and told myself how sorry I was that I had to deal with so many terrible things at such a young age. I told myself that none of it was my fault, and that one day I was going to have a great life.

When I looked over at the therapist, she was crying.

"I'm sorry," she said. "I'm so sorry for what happened to you, and I know that when you have someone tell you that and they're crying, that triggers emotions for you, too. But you need to know that I am truly sorry that those things happened to you. I want you to pretend that it isn't you now, and I want you to cry for that little girl who went through these things."

I pictured how much I loved my kids and children in general, and how the thought of a child being hurt bothered me so much. I cry for things I see on the news, but I would not cry for myself?

How young and innocent I was. How wrong it was that I had my innocence taken away from me on a daily basis. The verbal abuse is what ran though my mind the most, and the fear I lived with my whole childhood about these mean men.

"I want you to picture yourself at a time in your child-hood when you knew something was going to happen to you with your uncles," she said.

Of course, my mind went straight to that *Cat People* movie. Me, sitting on the corner of the bed in a tank top tied at the shoulders, with scrunchy elastic across the top, and my stringy hair.

"Tell her what you want to tell her."

"I'm so sorry that this is about to happen to you," I said. Then I fell apart. I just kept saying, "I'm so sorry. I want to protect you." The mother in me wanted to mother her. I could see what was coming, and there was nothing I could do to stop it. He was going to touch her, do things no child should ever even know about, and demean her with his nasty words. I wanted to scoop up the girl and take her far away, to turn back time and make it all different.

But the little voice that came back to me said, "I got this. Don't worry about me. You think I listen to what he says?"

"Even then, you knew you had to be tough," the thera-pist said. "Even at seven, you were never a child."

When I would say things like, "It was bad, but it could have been worse," or "Other people's problems are worse than mine," she would tell me that I needed to admit that my life was bad, that it was wrong what happened to me, and that these were my experiences, not someone else's.

I cried so hard that I couldn't stop crying . . . for days. That was also the time my migraines quit for good, and I know that was no coincidence. So much of what triggered my headaches were all these buried memories and fears and sadness lurking around in my brain. But now I would cry openly about it in therapy and feel sad for that little girl and not feel like I had to keep it all inside anymore. Everyone cries, so you all walk around looking like death for those first couple of weeks—breaking your addiction and dealing with your life all at once is something that could make anyone crack wide open, so there were grown men falling out crying all over the place.

The therapists never make you feel like you're on the clock, or like this is a job to them. At any hour, there's always someone to talk to who will listen and care, and you know their hearts hurt for you because there was a time when they felt like you feel. As the days went on, I felt stronger and more settled in. I learned to appreciate the "bubble" atmosphere there, where you don't have to deal with any normal life stuff, like grocery shopping, cooking, or constant phone calls. You're there to work on yourself, and the whole staff is there to make that easier for you.

So even though I still missed my family a lot, I knew I was doing the right thing for me and for them. I thought about what a better mother and wife I could be once I got my own issues worked out.

Bryan didn't understand that in the beginning. By the end of the day, I was so exhausted and talked out that I just didn't want to do any more talking. He wanted to be included on everything, wanted to know what I did every day and what I talked about, and I would say, "I've been in therapy for *eight hours*. I just don't want to talk about it."

At home, he was doing a great job of being Mr. Mom, and maybe I resented that a little, too. He's a better cook than I am, and he took off work that whole month to be with the boys. He didn't want any help caring for them; he wanted them to turn to him for all their daily needs, and they did. As much as I appreciated that later, at the time, I was jealous that he seemed to have it all so put together while I was the bad mom in rehab.

At my first hypnotherapy session, I just fell apart on this gorgeous woman's couch. She was a mom of two boys, too, so she understood when I told her how much I missed my kids and how lousy I felt about leaving them. We didn't get any hypnotizing done that day.

But the next session was different. She would count down from twenty, and I think I was out by about eighteen. She told me I was one of the easiest people she'd ever hypnotized, and I think that's because prayer is like hypnosis to me. I can be so deep in prayer that I lose the whole world around me.

Hypnosis didn't feel like what I expected. I still felt very aware of what was going on, but things were not in my control. To show me this, she told me to put out my hands, then told me she was putting a helium balloon in one hand, and bricks in the other. Right on cue, my one hand shot up in the air and the other plummeted. *What in the world?*

We would do different exercises. In the beginning, she asked me to write out a list of qualities I wanted to have: the "Ideal Tracy." When I was under hypnosis, she told me I was at the bottom of a staircase and I was walking up the stairs toward Ideal Tracy. As I took steps, she'd tell me all about that woman I was walking toward: she was fearless and kind-hearted and organized and a great mother. But for the first several sessions, all I could see was the back of Ideal Tracy. I couldn't get her to turn around and look at me. Finally I got her to turn around, which felt like an accomplishment.

Then came the "heart tour." She told me to pick someone to be my guide, and I picked Jesus (of course!). I was to picture both of us shrinking very small so we could take a tour inside my heart. But when we got there, it was filled with black tar and I couldn't see anything.

"I want you to find the sparkles," she said.

"There are no sparkles to be found here."

"There are sparkles. Look around."

"Seriously, there are no sparkles."

Well, I finally found some sparkles, and we headed to a place in my heart where people had taken things from me and I got to ask for them back. A place where people had taken my innocence, my pride, taken my feelings for granted. They all had to give those things back, because my guide Jesus was there to enforce it and protect me. Our way back out of the heart was totally different; the tar was gone, and it was so bright I covered my eyes.

As I came out of hypnosis, I turned to the therapist and said, "Seriously, it was hard to find those sparkles." She screamed with laughter.

You start taking these light-bulb moments for granted after a while, because you have them every day. It's like one big epiphany after another, where you learn more about who you are and why you are and what's holding you back. Kind of like living in Hawaii, where the weather is the same every day. "Oh, look, another beautiful sunrise. Another beautiful day." You get used to it, which is why it's fun to see the people who are newer and just "getting it." They're all running around journaling and breaking out of the gates ready to change the world, because they've just started to see everything differently.

I had a few more encounters like the one with the aggressive "thirty-five-pills-a-day" lady, so I brought it up in a group session one day. Someone was popping off about how much cocaine he did, and I got irritated.

"My addiction is not a scarlet letter," I said. "I'm not ashamed. Nor is it a medal. I don't walk around proudly displaying all my addictions. Why does it have to be one or the other? Why can't it just be something we did that we're not going to do anymore?"

I felt better after saying it, because I was tired of both extremes. It hurt to see people who were so ashamed that they could barely make eye contact, and to see others who seemed to be bragging about their problems.

After I'd gotten my grounding, I decided to challenge the speaker at a metaphysics lecture. He was talking about how we are all God. That there is no God except ourselves. "I disagree with that," I said. "I am not God. I think that's a comfortable idea for people who don't want to be held accountable to anyone but themselves. If they're God, they don't have to answer to anyone."

He stared at me. I'm not sure if anyone else had challenged him before. But it set the tone for what was to come. Later, he insisted that if we weren't told what to believe as children, our human instincts would lead us to metaphysics. Again, I raised my hand and said, "No one handed me a Bible and told me to read it when I was a kid. I found Jesus on my own."

"You really believe in the whole Jesus thing?" he asked.

I lit into him in a very sweet, southern way.

"I'll tell you what I believe," I said. "I believe the Bible and everything in it. I believe it took 1,200 years for Noah to build the ark. I believe that Elijah never died—he left this earth in a chariot of fire. I believe that Jesus was the son of God, and He was sent here for us, and He died at thirty-three and rose again three days later. I believe He's the only true living God and that He is alive today. I live my life with this belief, and I try to do the best I can with what the Bible says. I screw up and make mistakes, but I'm a good person who lives a good life according to Scripture. I believe there is going to be a rapture, and we're going to leave this Earth, and if you have accepted Jesus in your heart, you're going with Him to heaven. I believe that with all my heart."

"And what if you find out there is no Jesus and you lived your life based on a lie?" he asked.

"If I'm wrong, I've lived an amazing life and done all I know to do to be a good person. That's okay. But what if I'm right? Where does that leave you?"

He laughed. "You really want to go there with me, Tracy?"

"Bring it on," I said.

My poor friend sitting next to me about swallowed his tongue.

With big gestures and dramatic mannerisms, the speaker said, "So you mean to tell me this *Jesus* is going to come back to Earth and just take Christians to heaven . . . what about the billions of people in the universe who've never even heard of him?"

"It says in the Book of Revelation that before the rapture comes, every person in the universe will have heard the truth of Jesus Christ, so the rapture cannot happen until the word of the gospel has spread to every small corner of this Earth and everyone has had a chance to either accept or deny the truth of my Lord Jesus."

And he said, "Let's change the subject."

After the lecture a burly guy with a beard came over to me and said, "I believe everything you said. I grew up in a

Christian home and went to a Christian school, but for so long, I've felt that I disappointed God."

"He never left you," I said. "You left Him. Even when He is disappointed with you, it doesn't mean He stops loving you."

I went on to explain to him my view about God's grace. If my kids run across the floor in their socks and they fall down and start crying, I feel terrible for them. I pick them up, hug them, and tell them to not do it again because they could hurt themselves. The second time they do the same thing and fall down, I feel just as bad as the first time. I hug them and ask them did they not remember me telling them not to do that or falling just seconds ago? I help them up, and remind them not to do it again. The third, fourth and fifth time they do it and fall, I still feel bad. I know that it hurts, but I don't run over to them. In my heart I want to, but I feel that, by now, they must own the consequences of their actions and disobeying. I let them sit there and cry. As much as I want to go and comfort them, I don't. That's how I see God.

He always loves us and always sympathizes with us, even when He wants us to take responsibility for our mistakes.

It began to be clear to me: There was a reason for me to be there, aside from the obvious one. Yes, I needed to be there to heal myself—and the therapists were amazing and helpful in that regard—but I was also there to remind others that God hadn't forgotten them.

Actually, the therapists had to keep reminding me to

deal with my own stuff. Once I was past the detox stage, as usual, I wanted to help everybody else instead of worrying about myself. There were so many sweet people there. One girl, in particular, touched me. She was in group therapy with me, and when she arrived, her spirit looked like the Hunchback of Notre Dame. She was so dark and full of shame, but she had this blinding smile. You could just see that there was a very special person in there somewhere.

In one session, she told us that she had been in several mental institutions in the last ten years. She had even been told that she would probably die in a mental institution. Her life story was a lot like mine, maybe worse. When she was just in grade school, she had started cutting herself to try to get the "bad blood" out.

If I didn't have Jesus, that could have been me, I thought. I was so drawn to her because I felt like we were flip sides of the same coin.

I felt like Jesus was yelling in my ear, "Tell her what you see," so I interrupted the session to give her a message.

"Katy, you've been living a lie from the pits of hell. The devil has been trying to kill you your whole life, but God has such an amazing destiny for you. You need to see your future. Don't come in here with your head full of files about what your therapists and your parents have said about you. Don't walk in here and hand us this and say 'This is who I am.' Tell us who *you* know you are in your heart. Who do you believe God created you to be? Who do you believe you are?"

"Well, I don't believe I'm crazy," she said.

"You're not. You've just been told that for too long. But you have a clean slate now, to work through stuff and figure out who you're going to be."

She's an extremely smart girl, pretty and young, but it was as if the devil had put a black cloak over her.

"You've got to fight this," I said. "If you don't fight, he's going to win. It's a pretty big compliment if the devil is trying to aggravate you, because he can't be everywhere, so you must be a pretty important person for him to work so hard to keep you down."

She smiled then, and said, "I never heard that before."

When I told my story, she cried and said, "I'm so sorry for you."

"Katy," I said, "We are the same person. The only difference is that I have always had faith in Jesus and felt like I had someone to talk to."

I met people there with life stories that would break your heart: a woman whose father and brother were killed in a car wreck who lives with the nightmare of seeing their brains splattered across the dashboard; women who were brutally raped; a man who was forced to watch an intruder murder his sister. You see a lot of angry people in rehab, people who need to yell it all out. That's hard to take in the beginning, but pretty soon, you all become a family and you figure out what makes people tick, and what's behind the yelling. And that's when the healing begins.

My faith just kept growing the longer I was there. It really didn't matter that I was the only Jesus freak around; I decided to share my faith openly whenever it came up. One man who worked there told me he thought the life of Jesus was a "great story," and the Bible was a book of metaphors. "How do you believe in something you can't see?" he asked me.

"I want you to look out the window at the leaves moving on those trees. Do you believe that?" I asked.

"What do you mean?"

"You don't actually see the wind. That's what faith is. You can feel it, and you can see what it does, but you can't see it. You just know it's there anyway."

"But then, if there's a God, and He loves you so much, why did He let you get addicted to pain pills?"

"Because I have free will. I chose to take them."

"Why didn't God make you stop taking them?"

"Because He's not Hitler, and I'm not a robot. When you have a prescription, it's easy to justify to yourself that you really do need them every four hours, like it says on the bottle."

"This whole thing about you hearing from God . . . how do you know that you weren't just delusional from the pills?"

"Your wife . . . the first time she ever called you on the phone, she had to identify herself to you. 'Hi, this is Lauren.' But after a while, she didn't have to do that anymore. She knows your voice and you know hers. That's how it is with the Lord for me. I know the voice of the Lord like no other voice."

I don't know if I convinced him, but it was important to me to be adamant about letting him know that it was insulting to equate my relationship with Jesus to a hallucination caused by opiate drugs. There comes a point where logic can't go any further and you just need to take those last steps on faith alone. Some people have a very hard time with that, so it may have been easier for the man to imagine that my conversations with God were drug-induced, but I've been hearing from God since I was seven, and I sure wasn't on any opiates then.

Because I felt like most of the people there didn't understand what I believed or why, I did my best to explain that my faith isn't based on a bunch of judgmental thoughts and harsh rules. It's based on a relationship with God. So many of them had never heard about the loving God I know. They had heard about the condemning God, but not the God who loves them the way they are and doesn't expect them to be perfect. I sometimes think I was the first person to share that with them.

Seeing me there and knowing I had screwed up made it easier for them to believe what I was saying. Being around me and watching me go through so many emotions and seeing me continue to screw up every day made them realize that you can be broken and still have faith. They would see me break down and get mad and cuss and they'd expect me to be embarrassed, but I wouldn't be embarrassed because I'm not perfect and I don't believe God expects me to be. I think it was easier for them to hear me talk about God because they saw me as someone just like them.

After I'd been there for a month, I went home for Easter. My therapists thought it would be good for me to go home for a week, then come back and finish the rest of my recovery. When I came back to the center, it was familiar, not scary like it was the first time. I felt proud to go back and complete the treatment program. My track record wasn't so good for following through on things, and this time I was determined to do all I was meant to do.

Before I left to go home for a week, I went shopping and bought Easter baskets for my friends. I got a pretty china doll for Katy and left it with a nurse to give to her on Easter morning. When I got back, she told me, "You didn't even know I collect china dolls!" She looked completely different. She was standing taller in a bright yellow shirt, and her whole spirit was lighter.

Jason, another man who had become a good friend of mine, took me aside one day and asked me if he could talk to me about this whole "Jesus thing." Jason owns a chain of hardware stores and is a very successful businessman. I had talked about tithing, and he said, "Your husband buys into this?"

"Absolutely," I said. "Ten percent of everything we make goes to the church."

"But ten percent of what I make is a lot of money."

"Jason, it isn't yours to begin with."

"What if it turns out you gave it to crooks?"

"You pray about it, and you go to a church and see where you feel comfortable. They have to answer to God about how they use the money; God honors that you've given it to them even if they do the wrong thing with it."

Well, after I was talking to Jason for a while, Jesus said to me, "Tell Jason that I love him so much that his soul was worth you getting addicted to pain pills and being away from your kids for six weeks and having to go through rehab for this moment right now, for you to tell him about me and how much I love him."

I told him. And he got it.

It did feel worth it, everything that I had to go through to stand there and give these messages. Although I missed Bryan and the kids so much, I knew the Lord honored that.

Before I left, one of the employees asked if I was interested in coming back every now and then and helping with the spiritual counseling. I laughed and said, "That's sweet. A month ago, you all thought I was crazy." He said with a grin, "Yeah, but there are more of you coming in now." It was like it was the first time they realized that there were other clients coming through the program who shared my faith.

Coming out of rehab, I knew that the experience had been a test for me. It's one thing to be faithful and love God in your own little comfort zone, but another to be put in a situation where no one has the same faith as you and people in authority are telling you that your beliefs are wrong. Jesus always gave me the words to say, facts from the Bible that I didn't even remember reading. After all, He didn't just hang around with people who shared His beliefs, either. He hung out with everybody.

I was glad I had been adamant about what I believe. I think it was good for people to see that when someone says they have faith, it doesn't mean that he or she is without fault.

None of us were forced to be there, or to stay there. We had each checked ourselves in and could leave at any time, but we were enough of a family to keep each other on track and stop each other from giving up too soon. Being there was something I had to do for me.

The weeks that I was there were a tornado of emotions. Bryan and I argued a lot over the phone, both saying and doing things we didn't mean and that we would regret. Being away from your family is hard. Add on the worry and stress of the fact that I was in rehab, and that is truly enough to test any marriage. But one of the great things about God is that He can and will use your screw-ups in life to make you stronger.

The most amazing thing to me about being there was the fact that everyone there looked like me. I had a fear of going there and being "locked up" with a bunch of strung-out weirdoes who I'd have nothing in common with. I was so wrong. They were great people with great stories. Most of them, like me, had deep issues of hurt and neglect that they were trying to mask with drugs and alcohol. One thing I found out is that it takes a lot more courage to admit you have a problem and deal with it than to ignore it. After being there and learning so much, I really believe everyone could use a little rehab.

Our joke there was that the "outside world" started to look a lot more dysfunctional than the rehab world.

When we got phone calls from friends outside the center, they'd ask, "How are you?" in sad, sympathetic voices. We all knew that if we answered truthfully, we would tell them, "We're great. Actually, probably better than you."

I tell my friends only half-jokingly that it would do everyone good to "check out" for a month and check in. You have to be brave to take time out to deal with stuff you spend your whole life keeping busy to forget.

When I said my goodbyes, there were a lot of tears, but I was more than ready to go back to be with my family.

"Mom, I cried a lot while you were gone," Elijah told me.

"Me too," said Jacob. "I didn't want to cry in front of Dad because I knew he was worried, but I cried myself to sleep at night."

That should be enough to keep any mom clean. I never wanted to leave them again or have them worry about me.

The morning after I came home—and this sounds so corny, but it's true—it was like the whole world was brighter.

Everything looked so clear and sounded so clear. I thought, *These trees never looked so green.* A fog had lifted.

Sometimes you don't realize what your life looks like until you've been away from it for a while and had a chance to get perspective. There was so much from my childhood I had just been hoping would go away, and so many things I was just brushing aside every day. There hadn't been a day when I didn't have a headache, so I missed out on so many things, and I slept in too much. Now I'm completely off medication because I don't have anything to take medication for—ever since that day in rehab, I haven't had a single migraine ever again.

The difference in how active I am now, without the pain, is amazing. I get up early every morning and am not sidelined by headaches. My purse isn't a medicine bag anymore, and the kitchen drawer isn't full of empty bottles. And I finally feel like I walked it out like God wanted me to, finding real healing within myself instead of in a pill.

— Ten

I WASN'T PREPARED TO COMPETE IN THE MRS. Texas pageant again. I had competed both of the last two years, and both times, I was the third runner up. Before that, I hadn't been in a pageant since I was about seventeen. I didn't even know there were pageants for married women until I read about someone in the newspaper winning a state pageant. *After all these years,* I thought, *I wonder what it would be like.*

Kind of stressful, really. I tried to go on crash diets before the pageants, and to find just the right designer dress and suit. The day of the pageant, both years, I got whacked with terrible migraines and spent all the prep time just trying not to get sick. I would literally have to walk out of rehearsals to go throw up. Lots of my friends came and sat in the audience during the pageant, along with my family.

This year, I had toyed with the idea of trying just once more, but had pretty much talked myself out of it in rehab.

I had just spent six weeks crying my eyes out, going through detox sickness, reliving awful memories, and letting myself look pitiful. Plus, when you go through something like that, food is your one comfort. Mr. Goodbar was my steadfast companion through withdrawals. How was I supposed to be in a beauty pageant just a few weeks later?

My family talked me back into it. "You have to do it one more time," Elijah said. "I know you'll win this time."

Bryan could see that I was considering it. "If you're going to do it," he said, "I'll support you. But don't halfway do it. Don't wait until the week before the pageant and starve yourself."

So I started exercising again, going to the gym in the mornings. As much as I hoped to win, though, I was determined not to pressure myself. I did all I could to prepare myself mentally and physically, and I had to accept that I was not going to be in the best shape of my life. The kids reminded me every night when I tucked them in and prayed over them that I was always going to be the queen of this house.

Even though I lived just ten minutes from where the pageant is held, I still had to go and stay in the hotel with the other contestants. On Thursday, we all met and talked about why we wanted to compete in the pageant. Everyone has some kind of reason. Sometimes it's just the desire to have a special "girls only" weekend, or a desire to feel recognized as a beautiful woman. Some said they had entered pageants when they were younger and wanted to try it out again as adults. Several people gave spiritual reasons, saying that they had been through something difficult and wanted to prove that they had survived. Some had a cause they felt strongly about, and felt this would give them a better stage to speak it from.

When it came her turn to say why she entered, one Spanish woman who spoke broken English said very innocently, "Because I want to be the queen!"

We all laughed. Really, that's what it came down to. For all the other answers we could give, all of us wanted to be named a beauty queen for once. To wear that crown and feel special and pretty.

Later that night, we all did a photo shoot in our gowns. Then we went to our rooms and prepared for the next day.

On Friday, everything in the pageant has to be rehearsed. There's an opening number with dancing that is choreographed, but even the runway walks need to be practiced in order. Everyone needs to learn how to walk, and know where they need to be and when. That night, there's a party where we get to meet the husbands (they're not allowed to hang around during the rehearsals). When I would hear girls complain about the schedule, I would think about the way things were run at the rehab center. Just eight weeks ago, I woke up every day to find a piece of paper telling me where I needed to be every fifty minutes.

On Saturday everyone has breakfast, then interviews are

scattered throughout the day. Then we all rehearse on stage in the auditorium before going off to get dressed and ready for the pageant at 7:00 p.m.

This time, it was a totally different experience. I didn't feel like I had anything to prove to anyone, and I walked in already knowing I was a winner because of what I had just gone through.

My marriage is fantastic, my kids are great, I feel terrific, and we're going to Barbados on Monday, I thought. *I've done all I can. I'm clearheaded and healthy. I've already won, so whatever's going to happen from here will be fine.*

It was the first time I could say that and mean it. I had tried to convince myself before that I didn't really care about winning, but I was really sending myself other messages. I had so many crowns and trophies from my childhood pageants that I felt like I had something to live up to.

The morning of the interview, Bryan said to me, "Do your best. I love you and I'm proud of you, and remember that God and I already think you're a queen, and our crowns are much better anyway."

My platform was "Better, Not Bitter." It's the summary of how I try to live my life. Every one of us has problems and unfair things that happen. Some people blame their childhoods for everything that happens to them, and some people carry around a lot of anger and resentment about how much they've been wronged by an ex or a boss or whoever. Instead of being bitter, I choose to take my bad experiences and grow into a better person because of them, and I hope I can help other people do the same thing.

After the opening number, I prayed to the Lord, "Take me out of this whole equation. Take whatever I want out of it. If You're doing it to make me feel better because of what I've just gone through, don't. I feel good already, so if it isn't Your will to have me win this competition, don't do it to make me happy. If it is Your will and I'm supposed to win, let me know that it is 100 percent about You, not about me."

The judges narrowed it to the top five contestants, and I was one of the five. Then we each had to answer one more question. Mine was, "How do you define the ideal family?"

It was a great question for me seeing that is what I always wanted. I answered honestly that an ideal family is defined by love, not by some kind of formula for the right number of kids and the perfect house with a white picket fence. I also talked about how families come in all shapes and sizes, and some are even controversial. But I believe—and I teach my children—that we shouldn't judge other families but always look for the love in them. I answered, "As long as the people genuinely love and care about each other, that's an ideal family to me."

And that was the last part of the competition. All that was left were the awards. Because of the lights, I couldn't see my family in the audience, but I knew they were holding their breath for me.

"The winner of the preliminary for Best Evening Gown is . . . Tracy Elliott."

I won the first award! I was so excited, because I really hadn't been sure about the dress. Then they announced the winner of the interview preliminary . . . me! And most photogenic . . . me!

By then I was feeling a little awkward. Remembering how my husband and boys would cheer for me in past years when I wouldn't win, I was thinking that all the husbands, kids, and parents in the audience wanted their wives, moms, and daughters to receive an award.

"You might as well stay here, Tracy, because you also won Mrs. Congeniality and Contestant's Choice," the announcer said.

That was the sign I wanted. Of all the awards I could have won, the fact that the other women had voted for me meant the most. I felt like that proved I had been the person I was meant to be at the pageant, the person God intended me to be.

When they came to the third runner up in the announcements, I mentally prepared myself: "This is my spot." But it wasn't me.

Second runner up wasn't me, either. So it was down to just one other woman and me. I could hear some of the girls whispering behind me, "Tracy, you're going to win."

And I did.

"The new Mrs. Texas is Tracy Elliott," the emcee said,

vicious comments, and He said, "Nothing. You just go to the pageant and be yourself."

I often wonder how some people can be so judgmental about others. Are they so perfect and holy themselves? I prayed for the people who questioned my morals, asking God to give them some conviction about themselves and understand that His grace is forever. It's enough for everybody and everything. In the back of my mind, I felt sure that the people who were making these comments needed His grace as much as anyone else.

I suppose people expect me to feel ashamed of everything I've done, but you know what? I wouldn't be who I am today without those things. If I hadn't been a stripper, I wouldn't have met my husband, and my kids wouldn't have been born. That was no mistake. If I hadn't gotten addicted to painkillers, I wouldn't have gone to rehab and worked out all this stuff that's been sitting in my heart since childhood, and I wouldn't have been able to witness to so many people who've never heard God's word.

More than anything, I want people to know that they don't have to live out their "generational curses." No matter where you came from or what you've done, God wants you. No one is unforgivable, and no one is beneath His grace. The devil would love nothing more than for me to feel guilty for the rest of my life, but he can't make me ashamed of things I'll talk about and give God the glory for. God loved me when I was seven years old in old brown

and Elijah jumped about five feet in the air—I could s
him even with the glare of the lights.

I held up the "I love you" sign for Bryan and the bo
Everything else around us became a blur, and the mome
was as if my husband and my boys were the only people
the room. They were so proud.

I knew that the only reason I won was that it was Go
will. Without Him, I wouldn't have even had the sense to p;
ticipate, let alone relax and have a good time. I know there ;
reasons why I was supposed to have this title, and I pray tl
I will do whatever I'm supposed to do with it for God.

One of the things I'm looking forward to is visiti
orphanages. I'm planning a trip to the orphanage
Nicaragua with my crown and banner, telling the childi
that I was just like them. So many kids in orphanages h;
been abused; I would love to become a role model for the
to let them see that even if you grow up without a mom
dad, even if you have no money, even if you've been b
down and cussed out and made to grow up before your yea
God still has a calling for you. Kids just love the crown;
them if you're wearing rhinestones on your head, you
somebody important. And if that helps me get through
them, it's a great blessing.

Next, I will go to the Mrs. America pageant. Already, t
pageant world is bursting with gossip about how I w
once a stripper, so I'm an "embarrassment" to the contes
prayed and asked God what I'm supposed to do about th

clogs, He loved me when I was working in strip clubs, and He loves me still.

I thought about how far I'd come since those years in the Projects, which felt like a lifetime away. Sometimes I feel like I've lived enough for three people already. I choose to live differently now, but that doesn't mean I regret everything I've done. It took me a while to come to that point, where I could talk about things and not feel like a slug for not always having been Donna Reed. The experiences I had made me appreciate where I am today even more, and I believe I'm meant to share my truth to help people see that if I'm not embarrassed, they don't need to be, either.

Too many people live in fear of a vengeful God who looks for reasons to damn them to hell. That's not the God I serve. I know the Lord's heart like I know my own, and I know that in the time it takes you to take a breath, He's already forgiven you.

When I was seven, the Lord told me I was going to be on stage. I always figured he was talking about my pageants or the church plays. *Maybe I'd become a celebrity*, I thought . . . but that didn't happen. When I was stripping, I had almost accepted the sad notion that this was my stage. But it wasn't, either.

Then one day my pastor called on me to give my testimony in front of a couple thousand people. I nearly froze. I looked at my purple top and black pants and leopard-print clogs with big purple flowers on top and thought,

Great. I look *like a stripper who's found Jesus! Why did I buy these shoes, and why did I wear them today?*

I made my way to the podium and whispered to the pastor, "I don't know how much they can handle." He told me to tell it all . . . and I did. I told them about my parents, about the bad choices they made and the way I almost followed them to the grave because of my own bad choices. I told them about my uncles, how God lifted me up and saved my life again and again, and how He blessed my marriage and entrusted me with two sons who tell me they love me every day.

After I spoke, the pastor turned to the crowd and said, "Now, does anyone see my friend Tracy any differently after listening to her testimony?" It made me feel so comfortable to have a sort of "endorsement" from him in front of the congregation, in case anyone was unsure about how to judge me.

That day after I spoke, several people gave their hearts to the Lord. When I sat down, God said to me, "*This* is your stage." I almost laughed.

Being a Christian doesn't mean I don't sin. I figure I'm due for another sin about every thirty minutes. But I try and I listen, and I am obedient when the Lord talks to me. If He tells me to pray for the cashier at the grocery store, that's what I do. If He tells me to give my car to the church, I do it. And if He tells me to write a book where I reveal all the things you're not supposed to talk about in polite company, so other people can see that it's okay to talk about these things . . . I do it.

In writing this book and looking back over my life, I am honestly humbled by the mercy and grace God has shown me. As hard as I tried to run away, and despite all the mistakes I made, He never left me. That's not to say that He was never disappointed, but He was still always there.

Just like I don't believe that having faith in God means you are perfect, I also don't believe that it means you need to live a boring life and watch the world go by. I am very proud and passionate in my faith, and I take it with me wherever I go. I'm never ashamed or embarrassed of what I believe. Besides, once you've been naked on top of a table, what could embarrass you?

I always think it's funny when people try to be so composed when they worship. I give all I have. I figure that when I was drinking and partying all the time, I didn't halfway do that. I wasn't a wallflower in the corner at any party. Why would I sit down and be conservative about how thankful I am to God? Everyone worships differently, and I think that's great, but the thing that I find amusing is that sometimes the people who are so composed and reserved are the same people at the NBA games screaming their heads off. I guess it comes down to your priorities and your passion.

I believe that everybody has someone or something that they love unconditionally. Multiply that by a million and that is how much God loves you. No matter what! That's not something you ever need to keep quiet about.

o o o

Just before my grandmother died, she had asked my aunt to make sure I got that old wooden cabinet, the one thing still standing through all those years of chaos. My aunt always said that when I was settled, I could have it. She said she wanted to make sure nothing happened to it. Well, when Bryan and I moved to our home in Dallas, I assured her that I was settled and ready to take it. I couldn't wait to put it in our kitchen. I told Bryan how big and gorgeous it was. Funny thing, though, is that things look a lot different when you're seven.

My brother Bobby drove it to us from Georgia. When it arrived, it was this small, dented, plain old cabinet. It didn't go with any of our furniture, and it looked out of place . . . yet it was still the most beautiful thing in the world.

It found its home in my prayer room. I never had it refinished; I wanted to keep it just the way it was. It didn't need any fixing up to remind me of the miracle that it was even still standing, all in one piece.

One night, in the midst of a prayer, I glanced over at it and thought, *If this cabinet could talk* . . . What madness it had seen.

The Lord spoke to me then.

"You're both here and you both survived, and just like this cabinet, you remain unbroken."

— *Acknowledgments* —

As I finished writing this book, I looked back over my life, on paper, and smiled. I realized just how amazing the grace of God is! Sometimes we can't see things for what they are when we're in the middle of them. So, let me begin by saying how thankful I am for God's grace! Bryan, thank you for giving me the courage to relive my past, reminding me of my present, and sharing the hope of joy of my future! Jacob and Elijah, I'm so honored that God chose me to be your mom! To all three of you, I can't wait to see what the future holds for our family! One phrase comes to mind, "La Bella Epoch".

Bill Noble, thank you for encouraging me to tell my story (and "encouraging" Michael to listen)! Michael, you have a gift for seeing the potential in others! My prayer for you is that you take the time to look in the mirror and see the potential that is there! Thank you for all you've done! Jenna, I'm grateful that God put you in my life! You're more than the writer, you're my friend. You listen without judgment, and you write without hesitation! Jonathan Merkh, your integrity, compassion, and faith made this experience great! Your patience and understanding allowed my story to come full circle. To everyone at Thomas Nelson, thank you all, from the bottom of my heart! Jan and the girls at Dupree Miller, thank you for all you have done.

To everyone else who has been so encouraging during this process, there isn't enough time or space to thank you! You bless me! To ALL my friends in the ministry, thank you for being real examples of God's love! In a world where judgment and hypocrisy run wild, all of you show what it means to "practice what you preach".

One last thing. Thank you, God, for being God. You are much better at it than I am! Your way is the best way, and to my surprise, it's a lot easier when I listen to you. I should've learned that a long time ago. Although, if I had, this book would be a lot shorter and a lot less interesting!

39092 07567255 2

JAN 2 0 2010

ROCK SPRINGS LIBRARY
400 C STREET
ROCK SPRINGS, WY 82901
352-6667

RK 277.3 Elli
39092075672552
Elliott, Tracy.
Unbroken   MCO

ROCK SPRINGS LIBRARY
SWEETWATER COUNTY LIBRARY SYSTEM
ROCK SPRINGS, WYOMING